INTRODUCTION

QUICK WIN MARKETING is aimed at entrepreneurs and business managers who want to start, grow or revitalise a business and companies launching new services or products in the UK or Ireland.

The book is designed so that you can dip in and out seeking answers to your top marketing questions, as they arise. There are four sections to the book:

- Marketing essentials.
- Launching new services / products.
- Growing your business.
- Revitalising your business.

Marketing essentials is ideal if you are new to marketing, starting a new business or need to refresh your marketing knowledge. Find out here how to price services, set targets and develop a marketing plan.

Launching new services / products looks at identifying opportunities, valuing the market and protecting your idea.

Growing your business is a challenge many companies face. This section illustrates ways to grow a business, using both online and offline tactics. It includes online tactics such as ways to increase your web traffic and understanding YouTube for businesses. Offline marketing tactics explained include writing press releases and organising open days.

Revitalising your business is aimed at established companies that need a kick-start. This section provides tools and templates such as brand maps and SWOT filters. Learn here how to find new markets and win more pitches, as well as how to conduct surveys with potential and lapsed clients.

In addition, using the grid in the Contents, you can search for questions and answers across a range of topics, including: management, branding, research, innovation, pricing, promotion, sales and online.

And, where appropriate, answers cross-reference to other questions for a fuller explanation or more information.

Finally, as your knowledge and skill in marketing grows, you'll find a growing number of questions and answers – including comments and advice from other marketers – on **www.quickwinmarketing.com**. For more details on this website, see page 188.

Enjoy the book – I wish you lots of quick wins and success in your marketing!

Annmarie Hanlon
April 2009

CONTENTS

Search by theme:

Or search by topic:

Management

Branding

Research

Innovation

Pricing

Promotion

Sales

Online

using the grid overleaf.

MARKETING ESSENTIALS	Management	Branding	Research	Innovation	Pricing	Promotion	Sales	Online	
Q1 We've got a great idea, will it work?	☑		☑	☑					2
Q2 How do we take an idea and turn it into a business?	☑		☑						4
Q3 What market research do we need?	☑		☑						6
Q4 How do we create a business name?		☑		☑		☑			7
Q5 How do we get a logo?		☑		☑		☑			9
Q6 How do we brief a logo designer?	☑	☑		☑		☑			11
Q7 How do we price our products?	☑		☑		☑				13
Q8 How do we price our services?	☑				☑				15
Q9 How do we find customers?	☑		☑			☑			17
Q10 What are the 7 key ways to promote our business?	☑					☑		☑	19
Q11 What's the difference between sales and marketing?	☑								21
Q12 How do we create a mailing list?			☑			☑			23
Q13 How do we set sales targets?	☑						☑		25
Q14 How do we work out the sales leads needed to achieve our sales targets?							☑		27

MARKETING ESSENTIALS

	Management	Branding	Research	Innovation	Pricing	Promotion	Sales	Online	
Q15 What's in a sales plan?	☑						☑		29
Q16 How do we prepare for client meetings?	☑		☑			☑	☑		30
Q17 What's in a client proposal?	☑					☑	☑		32
Q18 Do we need a website?		☑				☑		☑	33
Q19 What FAQs does our website need?			☑			☑		☑	34
Q20 What is a blog?						☑		☑	36
Q21 How do we prepare a brochure?		☑				☑			37
Q22 Should we advertise and when, where and how?						☑			39
Q23 What is ambient marketing?						☑			41
Q24 What sales do online businesses generate?						☑	☑	☑	42
Q25 What's in a marketing plan?	☑		☑		☑				44
Q26 How do we develop a marketing plan?	☑				☑				46
Q27 How do we create a marketing budget?	☑				☑				48

LAUNCHING NEW SERVICES / PRODUCTS

	Management	Branding	Research	Innovation	Pricing	Promotion	Sales	Online	
Q28 How do we identify opportunities?	☑		☑						52
Q29 How do we decide which opportunities will work?	☑		☑						54
Q30 How do we research the market?	☑		☑						56
Q31 How do we value the market and assess demand?	☑		☑						58
Q32 How do we get the staff involved?	☑								60
Q33 How will our competitors react?	☑		☑						61
Q34 What are Google Alerts?			☑					☑	62
Q35 How do we launch new products or services?	☑					☑			63
Q36 How do we generate media attention?						☑			65
Q37 How do we win awards?						☑			67
Q38 How do we protect our idea?	☑		☑	☑					69
Q39 How does sponsorship work for smaller businesses?	☑					☑			70
Q40 What is viral marketing?						☑		☑	72
Q41 What is buzz marketing?						☑			74
Q42 How does sales promotion work?						☑			76

GROWING YOUR BUSINESS

	Management	Branding	Research	Innovation	Pricing	Promotion	Sales	Online	
Q43 How can we grow our business?	☑				☑	☑			80
Q44 How do we segment our business?	☑	☑	☑						82
Q45 How do we sell our products?	☑				☑	☑	☑		84
Q46 How do we sell our services?	☑				☑	☑	☑		86
Q47 How do we promote our online store?						☑		☑	88
Q48 How do we create a blog?						☑		☑	90
Q49 Why is our website not listed with search engines?						☑		☑	92
Q50 How do we get more website traffic?						☑		☑	94
Q51 How do we revamp our website?	☑		☑					☑	96
Q52 How do we get the best out of networking?						☑	☑		98
Q53 What are social networks?						☑		☑	100
Q54 How do we create LinkedIn profiles?		☑				☑		☑	101
Q55 How does Facebook work for businesses?		☑				☑		☑	103
Q56 How can we use YouTube?		☑				☑		☑	105
Q57 What is bluecasting?						☑			107

GROWING YOUR BUSINESS	Management	Branding	Research	Innovation	Pricing	Promotion	Sales	Online	
Q58 How do we write a mailshot?						☑			108
Q59 What should we include in newsletters?						☑			110
Q60 Where can we buy mailing lists?						☑			112
Q61 How many mailings should we send out?						☑			114
Q62 How do we organise an email campaign?						☑		☑	116
Q63 How can we monitor our competitors?			☑						118
Q64 How do we write press releases?						☑			120
Q65 What is a cuttings service?						☑			122
Q66 Where can we issue news releases online?						☑		☑	124
Q67 How do we organise open days?						☑			126
Q68 How do we podcast?						☑		☑	128
Q69 How do we get staff uniforms on a budget?						☑			130
Q70 Where can we get marketing help?	☑								132
Q71 How do we manage a sales plan to ensure that we achieve our targets?	☑						☑		134

REVITALISING YOUR BUSINESS	Management	Branding	Research	Innovation	Pricing	Promotion	Sales	Online	
Q72 How do we revitalise our business?	☑								**138**
Q73 Do we need a brand map?	☑	☑							**139**
Q74 How can we use a SWOT filter?	☑								**141**
Q75 How can we generate more business from existing customers?	☑						☑		**143**
Q76 How can we find new customers?	☑						☑		**145**
Q77 How do we fire customers?	☑								**146**
Q78 How can we find new markets?	☑		☑						**147**
Q79 How can we win more pitches?	☑						☑		**149**
Q80 Should we dump some products?	☑								**151**
Q81 How does mystery shopping work?			☑			☑			**153**
Q82 How do we survey existing clients?			☑						**155**
Q83 How do we survey lapsed clients?			☑						**157**
Q84 How do we survey potential clients?			☑						**158**
Q85 How do we survey our staff?			☑						**160**

REVITALISING YOUR BUSINESS	Management	Branding	Research	Innovation	Pricing	Promotion	Sales	Online	
Q86 How do focus groups work?			☑						162
Q87 How do we measure service quality?	☑	☑	☑						164
Q88 How do we maximise our presence at exhibitions?						☑			166
Q89 What are webinars?						☑		☑	168
Q90 How do we run webinars?						☑		☑	170
Q91 What is interactive marketing?						☑		☑	172
Q92 What is search engine optimisation?						☑		☑	174
Q93 What is micro-blogging?						☑		☑	175
Q94 How do we create case studies?						☑			176
Q95 Does Google AdWords work?						☑		☑	178
Q96 What are affiliate schemes?						☑		☑	180
Q97 Do golf days work?						☑			181
Q98 How can we share good news?		☑				☑			183
Q99 How can we create greater impact meeting new people?		☑				☑	☑		184
Q100 What are the top 10 ways to promote our business on a shoestring?	☑								186

MARKETING ESSENTIALS

Great ideas need landing gear as well as wings
C.D. Jackson

Q1   We've got a great idea, will it work?

It often takes 100 great ideas to produce one that truly works – Linus Paul, the originator of the Linux computer operating system, said, 'The best way to have good ideas is to have lots of ideas'.

But a great idea that becomes a product or service needs more than just your courage. To see whether your idea will work, you need to answer these questions:

- Does this product / service replace or improve an existing item or is it a completely new idea?
- What are the alternatives? Don't forget that DIY is often an alternative for services.
- If it is not a new idea, what is its uniqueness? What makes it special?
- Why is it needed now?
- Although you can see the need for the product, will people outside your friends and family buy it?
- Is the idea time limited (i.e., will it only last for a couple of months or years, or has it a longer life)?
- What will it cost to produce?
- How can it be delivered (i.e., by post, in person, online)?

How do you know that your answers are right? Conviction and self belief is critically important, but firm evidence is what you need to start a successful business.

If it looks likely that there is a genuine need or desire for the item, then you need to do some further research.

> **HINT**
>
> Don't ask people if they 'would' buy the product or service, as everyone responds to a hypothetical 'would' with 'of course, we would'. Instead, ask 'How likely are you to buy this?', or 'How likely are you to pay XXX for this service?', as the responses to these questions will generate real feedback.

See also:

Q2   How do we take an idea and turn it into a business?

Q3   What market research do we need?

Q82   How do we survey existing clients?

Q2   How do we take an idea and turn it into a business?

The best way to make something happen is to make a plan.

Start by looking at the timescale you are working towards. Do you want the product or service available in three, six or 12 months? Is there an exhibition or other event taking place where it could be launched? Does it need to be available before Christmas or some other key date?

Do you have the finances to support the idea for the first six to 12 months? If not, there are many different ways to generate funds. When the timescale and funding has been decided, list all the steps involved.

This checklist is adapted from the '7Ps of marketing':

Area	Checklist	Action
Product or Service	Is the product ready to sell?	Finalise product development.
Pricing or Fees	Has pricing been agreed? Does it cover overhead and profit contributions as well as cost of sales?	Agree pricing. Look at delivery costs.
Route to market	Will the product be sold directly to the end users or indirectly through another company (distributors)?	Develop website. Identify distributors. Engage sales team.
Promotion	How do you envisage the product being promoted? What is the budget for promotion?	Create a promotion plan (linked to sales targets). Set a budget.
People	Do you need staff or can you outsource various services?	Identify staff or other support needed.

Area	Checklist	Action
Physical evidence	Where services can't be seen, the physical evidence is important and includes meeting rooms, staff appearance and packaging.	Review and explore what physical evidence is needed.
Processes	How easy will it be to buy from you? Do clients have to wait a long time? Is everything 'joined-up'?	Ask friends to test-buy to identify any shortcomings.

HINT Allow extra time in your plan to manage external factors. For example, your suppliers may quote three weeks to manufacture and deliver but, during holidays, this could stretch to four weeks. Staff recruitment can also take longer than anticipated.

See also:

Q3   What market research do we need?

Q25   What's in a marketing plan?

Q26   How do we develop a marketing plan?

Q3   What market research do we need?

To start a new business, the critical question is whether there is a real opportunity. You may believe there is an opportunity but, before you start spending money, it's worth undertaking some research.

You need to know:

- What is the market size?
- Who are the main suppliers?
- Who are your future competitors?
- What is the value of the current market?
- Who are the key customers?
- What trends are taking place in the market?
- What is the best 'route to market'?

Spending money on research before starting a new business will save time and money in the months ahead – and may help you to avoid disaster.

See also:

Q30   How do we research the market?

Q31   How do we value the market and assess demand?

Q35   How do we launch new products or services?

Q38   How do we protect our idea?

Q70   Where can we get marketing help?

Q4   How do we create a business name?

Company names are often based on people or places. Companies based on family names include **Barry's Tea** and **Cadbury's** chocolate. Businesses named after their location include **Aer Arann** or **Armitage Shanks** sanitaryware from the Staffordshire village in England.

Where place names were not available or not relevant, a new breed of names evolved: the product category name. For example, **www.gadgetshop.com** sells gadgets online and **The Irish Pub Company** (www.irishpubcompany.com) specialises in the design and installation of authentic Irish pubs worldwide. Product category names can work if a company can obtain the name as early as possible.

Other business names have nothing to do with the company – for example, **Firebox**, another online gadget company. Names can be a concatenation of two words e.g. internet = international + network.

To develop your business name:

- Take a blank sheet of paper and divide it into four boxes.
- In each box, write one of these words: Values, Image, Uniqueness, Services.
- In *values*, list down all the things that are important to you, what really matters – e.g. personal service, efficiency, attention to detail, expertise.
- In *image*, list all the words you would like people to say when describing your business.
- In *uniqueness*, think about why you will be different – e.g. 24 hour service.
- In *service*, list what you will offer, all the variations of your products or service.

- Based on these words, find some friends and brainstorm to generate various names.

- Look at the names in lowercase and UPPERCASE.

- Check with the Companies Registration Office / Companies House to see if the name is available.

- Go online to see whether a suitable website address is available.

- Say the name out loud and check whether it sounds good.

- Put the names onto a wall in your office and leave them there for a few days and then decide which is preferred or which name grows on you!

Try and plan for the future. Lulu O'Sullivan of 4giftsdirect.com originally called her company 'Inter Teddy' but, as the company grew, so did the range of gifts and it out grew its name. Lulu commented, "I would have rather pre-empted this, as it is hard enough to build up a name, and then to have to start again isn't ideal. My advice would be to put the time into choosing your name and think ahead as to how the business might develop".

HINT

Great names start with A to G (people still index and A is first). There are rules governing business names, so check with the Companies Registration Office in Ireland (www.cro.ie) or Companies House in the UK (www.companieshouse.gov.uk).

See also:

Q5   How do we get a logo?

Q73   Do we need a brand map?

Q86   How do focus groups work?

Q5 How do we get a logo?

A logo is a symbol of the organisation's name and should last for some time. It should represent the company's values (professional, expert, creative, etc).

In terms of style, logos can be a form of the company name, like **Barry's Tea** (www.barrystea.ie) or Dublin-based web designers **Go2Web** (go2.ie).

A logo can be a combination of a device and the company name, like **Oak Tree Press** and **Enterprise Ireland** (www.enterprise-ireland.com).

An intrinsic part of a logo is its colour and different colours convey different meanings. For example:

Colour	Meaning
Red	Danger, excitement.
Blue	Safe, conservative, reliable, professional.
Green	Honest, trustworthy.
Purple	Luxury.
Grey	Safe, conservative, boring.

Think about how and where your logo will be used, which may include online on websites, banners or directories and offline on letterhead, business cards, brochures, posters and exhibition banners.

In addition:

- Think about photocopying and printing. Will it copy clearly?
- Should you use specific colours?
- Are any symbols unacceptable to your target audience?
- Will the logo stand out amongst its competitors?

Budget Tip

Printing in one colour is cheaper than two colours. Equally, printing in two colours is cheaper than printing in four colours or in special colours, like silver or gold. The most effective, memorable logos are developed in one colour and are very simple – for example, **Guinness** or **Chanel** perfume.

Q6   How do we brief a logo designer?

The **Institute of Designers in Ireland** (www.idi-design.ie) and the **Chartered Society of Designers** (www.csd.org.uk) in the UK are the professional bodies representing designers. You can search for a designer on their websites. Alternatively, many advertising agencies offer logo and brand development services and can also organise marketing literature.

To create a great logo, a designer needs information:

- Background: details about the company, why it started and what it offers.
- Customers: who they are and why they buy from your company.
- Products: facts on what the company offers, its range of products and services.
- Main competitors: who they are, their websites and examples of their logos.
- Brief requirements: where the logo will be used (online, offline or both).
- Budget: what you have available for the design – for smaller businesses, this can range from €500 to €5,000 depending on the designer and how many ideas you want.
- Timetable: what your timetable is and whether there are any specific dates to be met.
- Way of working: do you want to see initial concept designs which can be quite rough? Or are you interested in finished designs only?

Consider what other requirements you may have, such as setting up the letterhead, business cards, website concept and putting the logo onto disk – these may cost extra.

When Acutec (www.acutec.co.uk) was developing a new name and new logo, the company advised the designer that a great colour not much used by IT companies was pink, although on the back of many computers, the parallel port is a specific pink colour. Acutec gave examples in the brief submitted to the designer.

| **HINT** | If you are developing an online business, the colour of the logo needs to be 'websafe'. This means the colours selected will look the same, regardless of the age of the computer used. If a colour is not websafe, a vibrant green can look dull and potentially different on every screen. |

See also:

Q70 Where can we get marketing help?

Q73 Do we need a brand map?

Q7 How do we price our products?

Pricing is a critical issue in starting a business. The business must decide whether it is offering high quality products at a low price, which would be a *superb value strategy*, or medium quality products at a low price which is a *good value strategy*.

		PRICE		
		high	**medium**	**low**
PRODUCT QUALITY	**high**	premium	high value	superb value
	medium	over charging	average	good value
	low	rip-off	false economy	economy

It is essential to understand production and distribution costs when pricing products. A good value strategy is fine, but *all* costs must be covered. Even though they have now fallen again, rising oil prices in 2008 had an impact on delivery and distribution costs, which is why some companies are now quoting minimum order values or adding surcharges for transport.

Products have additional variables, for example:

- Product-form pricing: Different versions of the product are priced differently – e.g., **Pat The Baker Sliced Pan White** 800g is around €1.69 and **Pat's Stoneground Whole Wheat Brown** 454g is €1.96.

- Image pricing: The product can be sold at two different levels, based on image differences – i.e., the same product is packaged in two distinct ways, each having a different price tag.

- Location pricing: The same product is priced differently at different locations, even though the cost of offering is the same – e.g., seats are more expensive in cinemas in Dublin than in Cork.

| HINT | At the start, decide on your pricing strategy, as it is difficult to start with one strategy and to change dramatically as the business evolves. This is why some companies that create a very different product offering start a second business or new identity. Toyota and Lexus are both Toyota products, but exist as different brands and separate companies with different customers and different prices. |

Q8   How do we price our services?

Services are different from products. Buying a product involves more senses: sight, sound, smell, touch and taste. With services, often you can't see them, they don't make a noise or smell and you can't touch or taste. This means that you don't know what you're getting until you've got it. It's difficult to ask for half a haircut or half a legal contract and then agree to move forward if you like what you see.

With services, clients use price and physical facilities as the major cues to source quality. Potentially, offering superb value for money is a dangerous strategy, especially for services.

Services are priced based on individuals' time, the location of the service and any products involved in the process. Prices for professional services are often referred to as 'fees' and the more training and qualifications involved, the higher the fee. Services can be priced using various methods:

- Market pricing: Whatever the market expects – for example, a lawyer charging fees of €10 per hour would be perceived as potentially useless and perhaps unqualified.

- Customer-segment pricing: Charge different prices for different customer groups – e.g., lower rates for pensioners and students on certain days or lower entrance fees for members of an association, like The National Trust.

- Time pricing: Prices varied by season, day, or hour – e.g., peak and off-peak rates, discounts on quiet days.

For many non-professional services, the clients' options frequently include DIY, which means that making a sale is less about price and more about demonstrating that your service is a better alternative. Clients perceive greater risks when buying services so, instead of price, think about what guarantees you can offer.

To get your pricing right, find out your competitors' pricing strategies and identify the gaps. People will pay for better quality. Even in recessionary times, people still have money to spend, but they take more time deciding where to spend it.

> **HINT**
>
> Small businesses will never succeed if their pricing strategy is low. Larger companies have deeper pockets and can always offer lower prices; they even can give services away free if they choose. Smaller businesses must focus on better service and added value.

See also:

Q7 How do we price our products?

Q63 How can we monitor our competitors?

Q9 How do we find customers?

The first step is to identify your ideal customer or client. This may be based on geographical location, number of staff, size of business, number of outlets, budget or specific needs to be met.

Business to business:

- What do your clients look like? Are their directors old or young?
- What are their aims? To purchase new equipment or needing a service?
- What size of business? SMEs, large corporations or public sector?
- How many employees? Less than 50, more than 5,000?
- What type of business? Manufacturers, retailers, distributors?

Business to consumer:

- What do your customers look like? Living on their own or with a family?
- What are their aims? To buy a gift, a household purchase or needing a service?
- What size of budget? Bargain-hunter or discerning purchaser seeking value?
- What type of household? Large, small or varying?
- A specific health category? Hard of hearing, weakening eyesight?

Identifying your ideal customer makes it much easier to find them. Look for groups – for example, if your ideal B2B client is a manufacturer, find the manufacturers' associations. This will give you potential lists to buy, as well as PR opportunities.

The next steps are to create a marketing plan and to identify how to promote your business.

HINT	Always start with a precise group of customers rather than saying 'we sell to everyone'. It's much easier to sell to specific groups rather than to the entire world.

See also:

Q10   What are the 7 key ways to promote our business?

Q16   How do we prepare for client meetings?

Q26   How do we develop a marketing plan?

Q44   How do we segment our business?

Q10   What are the 7 key ways to promote our business?

The 7 key ways to promote your business are:

1. Presence.
2. Participation.
3. Direct to desk.
4. Sales team.
5. Dialogue.
6. Media relations
7. Paid-for promotion.

It is estimated that the average American sees at least 3,000 advertising messages a day. We estimate the average European's daily exposure to advertising messages to be at least 1,000. **Presence** is about your business getting noticed in a world where there is a constant visual battle. Ways to achieve presence include: 'ambient' marketing, literature, sponsorship, sales promotion, websites and online.

Participation is getting involved: from events outside your business, to public events hosted by a third party and those inside your business that you have organised.

Direct to desk is sending something from your business so that it lands on the individual's desk. The aim is to bypass any gatekeeper and get straight to the target. When the communication arrives, it should capture their attention and result in action.

People buy from **people**. The ideal sales team includes your own staff, favourite clients who generate referrals and other contacts or networking buddies.

Dialogue is communicating with your clients, establishing a two-way conversation and getting feedback. This includes blogs, podcasts and networking.

Media Relations is a planned and consistent effort to establish and maintain contact between an organisation and its target audience.

We used to talk about advertising, but this has changed and we now think of **'paid-for promotion'**, whether offline advertising in magazines or online using Google AdWords and other directories.

See also:

Q22   Should we advertise and when, where and how?

Q23   What is ambient marketing?

Q36   How do we generate media attention?

Q42   How does sales promotion work?

Q68   How do we podcast?

Q95   Does Google AdWords work?

Q11   What's the difference between sales and marketing?

Sales and marketing are often confused as being the same thing but they are two different processes.

Marketing is meeting your customers' needs profitably. It has also been described as 'matching your assets to the customers' needs'. It is a strategic process and involves looking at:

- Product or service offering.
- Pricing strategies.
- Promotion strategies and tactics.
- Routes to market, which may include direct selling.
- People needed.
- Processes that involve the customer.

Sales is part of the marketing process, within promotion strategies or routes to market. In some sectors, especially business to business, a good sales team is the main way for the company to communicate with potential customers and to manage existing customers.

Marketing comes first, as it is difficult to sell something that customers do not want or need. A good marketing team equips its sales team with leads, market intelligence and reasons why potential customers should select their company.

The role of the sales team is to:

- Make appointments.
- Meet potential customers to understand their needs and identify solutions.
- Prepare proposals.
- Deal with any questions.

- Ensure the sale takes place smoothly.
- Manage the customer relationship.
- Feedback marketing intelligence to the marketing team.

Companies can be sales-focused or marketing-focused. A sales-focused company aims to sell as much as possible – the danger is that they develop 'transactional' customer relationships – i.e., the customer makes a purchase and goes. This type of company is always seeking new customers and does not manage to build real relationships for long term value.

A marketing-focused company adapts its offering to the customer. It will consider the customer's potential lifetime value and how the company can work with the customer to meet their needs. The aim is to build a fan club, where the customer will contact their company whenever the need arises.

HINT

A marketing-focused company sees the sale as the start, not the end, of the customer journey.

Q12   How do we create a mailing list?

You can buy a mailing list or create your own. Start by identifying who you want to contact. Is it:

- A specific profession?
- Members of an association?
- Companies in a specific sector?
- People located in one area?
- People aspiring to own a particular product?

When you have decided who to contact, you need to identify the group. For a specific profession, you can contact their professional body, which may have a 'yearbook' or list of their members online. The same may be true for members of an association.

You can look at the lists and perhaps telephone a few people to check that this is the right group for you. If it is, you either can buy ready-made lists from the professional body or association, or make a few calls and create your own database. It takes longer to create your own database, but it may be more up-to-date than one bought off the shelf, and will allow you to create your fields for information that is important to you.

The online information may only include a company name, without named individuals. If you know the type of person that you want to speak with, you can call and ask for their name. When you call, it's essential to confirm that it's OK to send a letter introducing your company.

Getting a list of people in one area, such as Dublin or Cork, London or Birmingham can be obtained from an edited version of the Register of Electors sold by local authorities, which publish two versions: the full register and the edited register. The edited register contains the names and addresses of voters who have opted-in to receive direct marketing.

Other ways to build lists for retailers include:

- Running competitions where you gather contact and other information in return for prizes.
- Highlighting special offers for VIP customers and encouraging customers to provide their details in return for invites to preview evenings, discounts or early bird offers.

Stores, pop groups and companies wishing to promote specific events can use 'bluecasting' to build their mailing list.

HINT	Check that it's OK to call businesses or individuals. In the UK, see www.tpsonline.org.uk and, in Ireland, see www.dataprotection.ie. If you make a call, where an individual has 'opted-out', you can be fined or prosecuted.

See also:

Q57   What is bluecasting?

Q60   Where can we buy mailing lists?

A good example of building a mailing list is **www.loveanaga.com**, whose high-value prize competition runs until December 2009.

Q13   How do we set sales targets?

Sales targets are goals for the sales team (which may include you) to achieve. There are many ways to set targets:

- Based on last year's sales, plus 'a bit'.
- Based on last year's sales, plus contributions from new products or services that have been introduced.
- Based on a vision the company has to seriously grow the business.

Sales targets can be any number you like, but they need to be realistic and achievable. When you have decided the total sales target for the year:

- Take the total sales target and divide by 10. Although there are 12 months in the year, it's better to focus on 10 as some months can be slower, depending on your market sector. This is your *monthly target*.
- Work out your *average order value*. This may vary, so pick an average. If you don't know, work out the lowest sale you would be happy to accept.
- Take your monthly target and divide by the average order value. This is the *number of sales* you need every month to meet your target.
- How many repeat sales do you get every month from existing customers?
- How many existing customers might be lost in the next 12 months?
- How many new customers do you need?

Add the details to a spreadsheet like the one on the next page and share it with the sales team:

Area	Example	Your Company
What is your sales target for the year?	€1,000,000	
Divided by 10, this is the monthly target	€100,000	
What is your average order value?	€5,000	
How many average orders are needed to meet the monthly sales target?	20	
How many orders will be from existing customers?	2	
How many new customers do you need?	18	

Further refinements may be needed to adjust the targets, as some months may be quiet and others will be busy. Looking at last year's sales is a useful place to start.

See also:

Q14 How do we work out the sales leads needed to achieve our sales targets?

Q15 What's in a sales plan?

Q14 How do we work out the sales leads needed to achieve our sales targets?

Put the kettle on, get a calculator and, ideally, a spreadsheet. Start by thinking about the sales target for the year, or the amount of income you want to generate. You need to know:

- The number of average orders needed and how many of these are likely to be from existing and new customers.
- How many proposals or quotes do you prepare to win one sale?
- How many potential clients or customers do you speak to before you prepare a proposal?

Use this table to calculate the number of leads needed each month:

Area	Example	Your Company
How many average orders are needed to meet the monthly sales target?	20	
How many orders will be from existing customers?	2	
How many new customers do you need?	18	
How many proposals do you need to win one client?	1 in 3 (18 x 3 = 54)	
How many people through the door do you need to get one proposal / enquiry?	1 in 2 (54 x 2 = 108)	
No of leads per month =	108	

HINT You can reduce the number of leads needed if you can improve conversion rates or ask more questions ('qualify your potential customer') before preparing the proposal.

See also:

Q13   How do we set sales targets?

Q17   What's in a client proposal?

Q15 What's in a sales plan?

A sales plan can be as complex or as simple as you like. We have found that a simple plan is more likely to be achieved.

Sales is all about activity. To generate sales, you need to be active!

The table below shows a simple plan. Enter the number of clients needed, with the number of leads and your planned activity to generate the leads.

Area	Your plan - forecast	Your plan - actual
Number of new clients needed		
Number of leads needed		
Activity to generate leads		
Activities this week		
And next week?		

It is useful to compare how the sales plan is progressing at the end of each month – and to revise it as necessary.

HINT Planning for the week ahead – and for the following week – helps to focus the mind and makes it easier to achieve targets.

See also:

Q13 How do we set sales targets?

Q16   How do we prepare for client meetings?

Before the meeting, consider your agenda and what you want to achieve. This may be:

- To find out more about the company?
- Their needs?
- Whether they have considered other solutions / alternatives?
- Why now?
- What's keeping them awake at night?
- Why have they asked you to meet them / agreed to meet you?
- What is the company's greatest challenge right now?
- What difference will it make if you go ahead with this work?
- Why is that important?

Questions you can ask at the meeting include:

- Can you tell me more about (situation or issue)?
- How long has this been happening?
- Why do you need to do something now?
- How much has the company spent on this so far?
- How many clients has the company lost as a result of (not having, doing etc) this?
- What will happen if the problem isn't solved?
- Does this matter?
- Can you quantify the problem in monetary or time values?
- Is there anything else?

Don't forget that the potential client has an agenda too, so you need to understand what they want to achieve. The client's agenda may be:

- To find out what you can offer.

- To explain their situation.
- To get free advice.

Plan what happens at the end of the meeting and agree actions, which may involve meeting again, preparing a proposal, meeting colleagues or, potentially, walking away.

> **HINT**
>
> If the buyer is too enthusiastic, there is a potential challenge! They may be information-gathering and picking your brains – beware and ask questions to explore why something is of interest and how it will help.

See also:

Q17 What's in a client proposal?

Q99 How can we create greater impact meeting new people?

Q17   What's in a client proposal?

Sometimes, for more complex or higher value work, you need to prepare a proposal rather than a simple quote. A proposal is usually several pages long (although not so long that people won't read it), should be easy to read and could be emailed or posted – or both!

A good proposal includes paragraphs about the following:

- Your understanding of the company's issues.
- How your company can add value.
- Why you are different and what else you can bring to their business.
- How you will measure success.
- Testimonials from happy clients and examples of awards.

The proposal can be presented as a document that is either printed and posted or emailed. When sending documents by email, try and print it first as a PDF (Portable Document Format) using Adobe Acrobat or similar. By converting to a PDF, your presentation style, formatting and images will be preserved and you can send a smaller file, which is often appreciated because it reduces download time.

You may also consider a PowerPoint slideshow that highlights the key points. Alternatively, why not go for a video email introducing your emailed presentation?

HINT

People have different learning styles, so try to ensure that the proposal is not all words! Images or diagrams can help to appeal to different folks. See www.vark-learn.com for a guide to learning styles.

See also:

Q16 How do we prepare for client meetings?

Q18   Do we need a website?

The first thing we do, when we hear about a new company, is to visit Google and check out the company's website. We use it as a reference point to see whether they look like the sort of company with whom we want to do business.

Today, a website is essential. It works 24/7, when you're asleep or when you're not in the office, all the time providing useful background on your company. Your competitors all have websites that potential customers can visit, gather information and make decisions.

Websites are often a more formal presentation of a business and, although there is work at the start to create content, when created, the key pages do not usually change. The home page and news pages may change, but the remaining pages are likely to remain static.

> **HINT**
>
> Make it easy to get in touch and ensure contact details are shown on every page. There is a legal requirement to show the company's registration number, registered office and its directors somewhere easily accessible on the site; in addition, contact details, in terms of postal address / phone etc, must be shown on the site too – though many sites still only give a contact form.

See also:

Q19   What FAQs does our website need?

Q20   What is a blog?

Q49   Why is our website not listed with search engines?

Q50   How do we get more website traffic?

Q19   What FAQs does our website need?

FAQs, or Frequently Asked Questions, used to appear on every website. As web users have become more savvy, this has evolved and these questions usually appear at the end of a page under specific headings.

Key questions that retail websites need to answer include:

- Delivery details.
- Information on returns.
- How secure is my credit card?

These details can be contained within a 'shopping with us' section.

An 'about us' section may answer questions and give the buyer greater comfort from knowing more about you. It's easier to buy from a person than a faceless company and this can be enhanced by including testimonials from happy customers.

Companies selling services need to provide credibility and the 'about us' section is likely to contain answers to questions including:

- Who are you?
- What can you do for us?
- Why should we choose you?

To answer these questions, it is a good idea to include details of the directors and key staff, any awards won and accreditations held. Service companies' websites should include information about their clients but, sometimes, sharing client names is a concern for service businesses. Also, some clients will not give their permission for the work to be broadcast. In this case, provide quotes without names to illustrate the sectors in which the company operates.

Other FAQs can be all those questions that you receive by telephone, whether it is 'where are you based?', or 'can we collect?', or 'what are your opening hours?'. All these subjects can be contained in the website, which saves your business time and money, by avoiding staff repeatedly answering the same questions on the phone or by email.

HINT	Don't forget that, if you are recruiting, a good place to advertise the vacancy and include more information is on your own company website. Then, when callers telephone requesting information, they can be directed to the website.

See also:

Q50 How do we get more website traffic?

Q51 How do we revamp our website?

Q20   What is a blog?

A blog is an online journal that may be updated daily, weekly or, in some cases, hourly. Many companies have both a website and blog because a website is a formal presentation of the company and a blog is a less formal, more interactive form of communication. Blogs are said to show the human side of a company.

When Microsoft allowed its developers to let techies know what they were doing, challenges they encountered and generally to interact with the IT community, the volume of hacking into its websites was reduced. No longer seen as a secretive unapproachable company, the Microsoft technical team were seen as ordinary people dedicated to IT.

Five years ago many companies did not have a website. Today it is unimaginable to consider a serious company without a website. In five years' time companies without blogs will be considered in the same way. Some newer companies are making a technological leap and creating a blog, rather than a website.

Similar to a website, there is space within a blog to incorporate sections such as about us, testimonials, contact and products. The main focus of a blog is the regular update facility, which can make a blog easier to find in Google than a new website.

If you are considering developing a blog, you need to consider:

- Its purpose – why does it exist and what difference does it make?
- Who will maintain it?
- How long will this take?
- How will we promote our blog?

See also:

Q48   How do we create a blog?

Q21   How do we prepare a brochure?

Do you really need a brochure? Usually, when we receive brochures, we flick through them and then file them – in the recycling bin! It is rare that we keep the brochure to refer to at a later stage.

However, in some sectors, a brochure is an indication of the company's size, abilities and is necessary to get a foot in the door of a potential customer. Unless you have fantastic creative talent in-house, opt for a graphic designer who can prepare a professional brochure that will give a good impression of your business.

The designer needs information from you which includes:

- Background to the company.
- Clients: who they are.
- Service: what you provide.
- Your main competitors.
- Aims: what you hope to gain from the brochure, how you will use the brochure, whether it will be posted or personally delivered.
- Budget: how much can you afford to spend on the brochure, any photographs, numbers required.

Get the sales team involved in the process. What questions are they asked frequently and what information do they need in the brochure? This needs to be finely balanced with giving examples or case studies showing why your company should be selected by the customer.

If you need fewer than 100 brochures, think about digital printing. The unit cost is higher per brochure, but the overall cost is lower – and you don't end up with thousands of out-of-date and unusable brochures mouldering a cupboard.

Photographs can be a challenge. If you don't have great in-house photos or images that you can use, there are websites where you can buy royalty free photos from as little as $5 per image.

HINT

Think in 'fours' when creating a brochure, as printing starts with four pages, then eight etc.

See also:

Q70   Where can we get marketing help?

www.istockphoto.com iStockphoto is an online image library generated by users, with over 3 million royalty-free stock images for as little as $1 each.

Q22   Should we advertise and when, where and how?

Advertising works. It builds brands and ensures customers remember your name. It is a great way to talk to existing and potential customers.

The key to success is regular adverts, because one-off adverts rarely work. To advertise on a regular basis means allocating a budget and planning all adverts over a twelve month period.

Advertising is more effective for business to consumer (B2C) than for business to business (B2B) companies. B2C usually have larger numbers of customers, whereas B2B may have fewer than 100 clients. If you have hundreds of customers, communication via direct mail could be very expensive and it may be better value to advertise. Equally, placing an advert and hoping your 100 clients may spot the ad is probably too expensive to justify. B2B can build brands and talk to clients using direct mail or PR instead.

Some of the most successful advertising we have seen is in parish magazines, local publications that are less expensive to advertise but read by all to obtain the local news. Specialist publications are another way to communicate with a specific target group of customers. There are many amazing publications available and local libraries may be able to obtain copies.

Local radio is another way to contact a local group of customers and can be very cost-effective. Historically, a rule of thumb for selling new houses was to get 12 people through the door to sell one property. Getting 12 viewers could take many weeks and the usual approach was newspaper advertising. A house-builder based in one central location used local radio, which was so successful that at least 20 people visited every single weekend and also created greater awareness of the company.

HINT Make sure all staff know about the planned advertising programme, so they are ready to respond to enquiries.

See also:

Q12   How do we create a mailing list?

Q24   What sales do online businesses generate?

Q47   How do we promote our online store?

Q95   Does Google AdWords work?

Q23 What is ambient marketing?

Ambient marketing is 'in place marketing' and means using the surroundings to promote your products or services.

Translating this into a practical use for businesses, it is about reminding visitors, whether they are potential or existing clients, potential staff, shareholders or other stakeholders, about your brand. Sometimes, you can visit an office and not be clear where you are – it looks like any of a million other offices. Ambient marketing captures ownership of the brand and shouts about this to visitors.

Ways to generate ambient marketing include:

- Ensuring staff are wearing the brand, the brand colour, or a pin badge bearing the logo.
- Looking at the brand colour and make sure this features in your reception area or meeting rooms.
- Bringing notepads bearing your company brand into meetings in other venues.
- Obtaining a pull-up exhibition stand to use as a back-drop at meetings.

The key is to promote your brand and company identity inside your building.

Budget Tip

A cost-effective way to promote your brand colour in a meeting outside your office is to bring a box of biscuits in your company colour into the room. It adds a smile to the meeting too!

See also:

Q69 How do we get staff uniforms on a budget?

Q24   What sales do online businesses generate?

Online businesses can generate significant incomes, depending on the product offering, the number of visitors to the site, the conversion rates of visitors to buyers and the average spend of buyers. Typical conversion rates are around 1%. Another factor is whether the company offers customers other options to buy such as in store, via catalogue, etc.

Some examples:

- A niche travel company gets around 10,000 visitors a month, over half via Google, of whom 1% place orders, with an average order value of €500. This company generates around €50,000 per month.

- An online shop (which also has a physical shop) gets over 2,100 visitors a month, of whom 3.5% place orders, with an average order value of £100. This company generates around £7,500 a month.

- An internet-only shop gets over 6,000 visitors a month, of whom 3.5% place orders, with an average order value of £58. This company generates around £12,500 per month.

What sells on websites?

- Chore or repeat purchases.
- Items which are not too complex.
- Items which are easy to buy.
- Items which do not need to be seen first.
- Price competitive or added value.
- Items which can be easily packaged and despatched.

HINT	For online businesses to work, the shopping process must be easy. Ask a friend to 'mystery shop' your own online business and see how well it works.

See also:

Q81   How does mystery shopping work?

Q92   What is search engine optimisation?

Q95   Does Google AdWords work?

Q96   What are affiliate schemes?

www.go2web.ie

Q25   What's in a marketing plan?

A plan takes a company from A to B and gives a company focus, shares actions between staff and ensures that tactics are agreed in advance, rather than on a whim.

We usually look at a marketing plan in three stages:

- Strategic review: where are we now?
- Marketing objectives and strategy: where are we going?
- Marketing action plan: how do we get there?

The strategic review should include:

- Market research information: statistics and details about the overall market.
- In-depth background: opinions from key players, industry associations and noteworthy publications.
- Competitor intelligence.
- Feedback from customers.
- Strengths and weaknesses inside the business.
- Opportunities, trends or threats outside the business.

The marketing objectives and strategy are created after the strategic review has been considered and should include:

- Objectives for the future of the business.
- Strategies for products and services, pricing, promotion and routes to market.

The marketing action plan is the stage that everyone enjoys as it's all about tactics. Because it's so enjoyable, some companies wrongly start with this and then try to create tactics to sell products, rather than tactics that meet the customers' needs, which should have been identified during the strategic review.

Your marketing action plan should include:

- Plan for the year, list of all actions, person responsible and when the action will be carried out.

- More details to explain the actions, so the individual member of staff can take the plan and get started.

- A budget, showing the amount required to carry out the actions.

HINT

The marketing action plan should be shared with all staff who need to implement the action.

See also:

Q11   What's the difference between sales and marketing?

Q26   How do we develop a marketing plan?

Q26   How do we develop a marketing plan?

It is useful to nominate one person to be in charge of the process – otherwise, planning usually fails. Set a timescale for each part of the process. Marketing plans can be rushed, but it usually takes time to gather market intelligence and develop ideas. Here is a guideline:

Stage	Timescale
Strategic review: where are we now?	3 to 6 weeks
Marketing objectives and strategy: where are we going?	1 to 2 weeks
Marketing action plan: how do we get there?	2 to 5 weeks

Strategic review: where are we now?

This stage involves research inside and outside the business. Looking inside the business involves reviewing the products, pricing, customers and promotion methods to see what works and what doesn't. A good place to start is to speak to customers and get their opinions.

The review outside the business includes looking at competitors, the overall market and future trends. This may involve speaking to industry associations and gaining their opinions, as well as 'mystery shopping' and gathering information from competitors.

When all this information has been gathered, the company can identify its strengths and weaknesses inside the business and highlight any opportunities or threats outside the business.

Marketing objectives and strategy: where are we going?

This stage involves getting the management team together and finding out what people want to achieve, where they want to take the business. The easiest way to do this is to write down a list of goals or objectives that each person wants. Share the objectives and create a combined list.

Take the combined list and develop it so that the objectives include an 'achieve by' date. It is also important to agree strategies for the product offering; is it the same or different? Access to the product: will it be via store, online or other? Pricing needs to be agreed.

Marketing action plan: how do we get there?

When the objectives have been developed, the company can list the actions needed to meet these objectives. This is called the Action Plan and should be shared with all staff who need to implement the action. From this plan, a budget can be created, showing the funding required to carry out the actions. It is important to monitor your plan on a regular basis – both against objectives and against budget.

HINT Activities in your marketing plan should always be linked to sales targets so that, if you cannot afford to fund all your activities / objectives, it will be easy to prioritise them.

See also:

Q27 How do we create a marketing budget?

Q81 How does mystery shopping work?

Q82 How do we survey existing clients?

Q27   How do we create a marketing budget?

There are four ways to set a marketing budget, based on:
- Percentage of sales.
- Comparison with competitors.
- What the company can afford.
- Achieving the objectives set out in your marketing plan.

Percentage of sales

Historically, a marketing budget was set as a percentage of sales. Typically, this started at 2% but could increase, depending on the company's aims and its sales turnover. Small companies may need larger percentages of sales to have an impact on the business.

Comparison with competitors

Looking at what your competitors spend, making an estimate of their budget and setting a similar budget for your business is another way to set a marketing budget.

What the company can afford

This is the budget formula that many small businesses adopt, identifying what they can afford to spend on marketing in a year and basing their marketing budget on this amount.

Achieving the objectives set out in your marketing plan

When you have agreed your objectives, list out all the expenses associated with each. Create a budget based on achieving all your objectives. This may mean raising additional finance.

Clearly, the best way to develop a marketing budget is to base it on achieving your objectives (otherwise, why set objectives?). However, affordability may be an issue and you may need to cut your cloth accordingly – but, at least you will know in advance that you won't be able to achieve all your marketing plan objectives and so you will have to prioritise (or re-think your objectives).

See also:

Q26   How do we develop a marketing plan?

LAUNCHING NEW SERVICES / PRODUCTS

If there's no challenge, there's no opportunity.

Q28   How do we identify opportunities?

Opportunities are outside the control of the business. They may be generated as a result of new legislation, political, environmental, social, technological, economic or demographics changes. As our lifestyles change, more opportunities arise. Fifty years ago, people would not have paid for bottled water and now we are seeing a new trend where 'tap water' is becoming popular again. Is there an opportunity to provide branded water jugs?

To find opportunities for your business, you need to gather information inside and outside the business.

Inside the business, you can talk to staff and explore any ideas they have from speaking to clients. How often do they say to clients, 'I'm sorry we don't do that?'. Have a brainstorming session with staff to identify new possibilities.

Outside the business, you can contact your trade or professional association and find out what legislative changes are planned in the future. How do these changes impact on your business and could they result in new product or service ideas?

Speak to clients and identify their future needs. Clients often think of new ideas as they are the users of the product or service. But, unless asked, they may keep these ideas to themselves.

Talk to suppliers and find out what changes they have noticed in the market and in customers' tastes. If you sell products, the suppliers often get previews of new products before they are widely promoted. Whilst services are different, their suppliers may see new ways of working that provide opportunities.

> **HINT** Lapsed clients can be a useful source of information about opportunities, since they may have lapsed because they needed something you could not provide.

See also:

Q29 How do we decide which opportunities will work?

Using a decision matrix is the best approach to deciding which opportunities are likely to work. It will help clarify which ideas will generate profit for the business and those that are quick to market.

The decision matrix below is a guide and can be amended to meet your business needs. Take all the ideas and potential opportunities open to your business for the next 12 months and list them in the first column.

In the second column, score the success probability within a timescale – for example, the next 12 months. Allocate 12 points for opportunities that are probable within the next month; 11 points if in the next 2 months; 10 points if in the next 3 months; and so on.

In the third column, rate the attractiveness of the opportunity. Attractiveness may be measured by profitability, entry into new markets or other ways. Allocate 12 points for very attractive, down to 1 point for less attractive.

Opportunities	Success Probability	Attractiveness	Total score
EXAMPLE Branded water jugs	6 points – could get to market in 3 months but other manufacturers already able to supply this.	10 points – attractive, as this would take us into the restaurant market.	16
EXAMPLE Change in legislation	8 – will happen in 10 months' time, so time to plan.	10 points – attractive, as this would take us into airports and ports sector.	18

Add the total scores and identify which opportunities are rated the highest. To make sure you don't get carried away, ask a few colleagues to do the same exercise and then take your average scores. Some ideas may be attractive in the next 12 months' and others may be great opportunities for the longer-term.

HINT

If you cannot score an opportunity, this means more research is needed.

See also:

Q28 How do we identify opportunities?

Q30 How do we research the market?

Q30　How do we research the market?

Many industry associations and government bodies produce reports that are useful starting places to research the market. The **Irish Internet Association** (www.iia.ie) contains reports on online shopping trends, broadband statistics and information about online advertising format trends.

For statistics, see **www.statcentral.ie** for Ireland and **www.statistics.gov.uk** for the UK. Both include information about:

- The economy.
- The environment.
- People and society (population, births, deaths and marriages, health).
- Social conditions (housing and households, education, crime and justice, information society).
- Business sectors (agriculture and fishing, construction, industry, services, transport, tourism and travel, science and technology).

Government websites such as **www.idaireland.com**, **www.gov.ie** and **berr.ecgroup.net/Browse.aspx** contain reports and background into sectors such as pharmaceuticals, ICT, medical technologies, international financial services and engineering.

Online directories including **Yellow Pages** (www.yell.com), **Golden Pages** (www.goldenpages.ie) and others – **www.mind.ie** and **www.browseireland.com** – can help with quantitative research, such as the number of companies in certain sectors and locations. Search engines can also provide useful information.

News articles for research into specific companies are available from many sources such as the **Marketing Institute of Ireland** (www.mii.ie) and national newspapers.

HINT Explore your local library, as you can often get access to market research and business reports that you can read for free.

See also

Central Library, ILAC Centre, Dublin 1 centrallibrary@dublincity.ie

City Business Library in London

www.cityoflondon.gov.uk/corporation/LGNL_Services/Leisure_and_c
ulture/Libraries/City_of_London_libraries/cbl.htm

Westminster Reference Library in London
www.westminster.gov.uk/libraries/findalibrary/westref.cfm

www.keynote.co.uk

www.mintel.com

www.snapdata.com

Q31   How do we value the market and assess demand?

Some market research reports contain estimates of market values. Industry associations also provide reasonable estimates.

If these sources are not available, you can:

- Identify the largest companies in the sector.
- Visit their websites and download their annual reports where available or obtain their figures from the **Companies Registration Office** (www.cro.ie) in Ireland or **Companies House** (www.companieshouse.gov.uk) in the UK, which make a small charge.
- Add all the turnover figures together to get an idea of the value of the larger end of the market.
- Add 20% or so to get a reasonable estimate of the market value.

This method is not foolproof and should be checked through conversations with industry associations, which may have access to more accurate market value estimates.

Assessing demand depends on the product or service. Sometimes, a product or service is generated due to political changes on issues such as the environment. Every great product exists because there is a challenge needing a solution! Without a challenge, there is no opportunity.

Consider these questions:

- Does the product or service already exist?
- Is it a growing market?
- Is it a crowded market or is there room to breathe?
- If it doesn't exist, is there a good reason why not?

- What are the alternatives or how do people cope without the product at present?
- Who are the customers and how can they be accessed?
- Is the product desired and acceptable?

The next stage may be to conduct focus groups or surveys.

See also:

Q84   How do we survey potential clients?

Q86   How do focus groups work?

www.keynote.co.uk

www.mintel.com

www.snapdata.com

Q32   How do we get the staff involved?

Engaging staff in new product development is critical to its success. Staff often have great ideas for new products but are rarely asked for their opinions.

To get staff involved, you can hold a competition announced in meetings or lunches with the theme: 'If you were MD for a day, what new products or services would you introduce?'.

A lunch is a great way to promote the idea. It should include details about:

- Why the company is seeking new products.
- What difference new products will make to the company.
- What the timescale is.
- What the reward will be.
- The process.

After the meeting, allow staff to think about ideas for two weeks. All ideas should be submitted to one person to collate. The ideas can then be grouped by theme. Smaller groups can be allocated to specific themes to investigate the real potential of the ideas.

Keep people updated through newsletters, the intranet or even a dedicated Facebook page.

 HINT At the start, don't limit the team with lots of restrictions! Allow people to brainstorm and to be creative.

See also:

Q85   How do we survey our staff?

Q33　How will our competitors react?

Different competitors will react differently to your new product launch. Some will take no action, some may review or extend their own products, some will reduce prices and some may talk badly about your products. The key issue is to be prepared before launching new products or services.

To manage any reactions, you should list all your main competitors and:

- Identify all the new products they have launched in the last two years.
- Discuss with the sales team whether the competitors are likely to launch any new products in the next 12 months.
- Brainstorm all possible reactions.
- Agree contingency plans in case the reactions occur.

HINT

It is useful to prepare a selection of press releases to counter any claims about a new product.

See also:

Q34　What are Google Alerts?

Q63　How can we monitor our competitors?

Q34   What are Google Alerts?

Google Alerts is a free monitoring service for news, web pages and groups. After specifying your search terms, Google will notify you by email if it finds results matching your criteria.

Google Alerts can be used to:

- See where your name or company name is mentioned online.
- Keep tabs on competitors.
- Follow a specific market trend.

You can choose how often you want to receive alerts: once a day, as it happens or once a week.

Managing your alerts page will allow you to create, verify, edit and remove any alerts. To access this feature, you will need to create a Google account.

HINT

Create Google Alerts for your own company and for yourself, so you can see what is being said about you and your business online!

See also:

www.google.co.uk/alerts?hl=en

Q35   How do we launch new products or services?

New product launches start with an idea and then a plan. Sometimes, great products fail at the launch stage because one element of the plan was missed.

A successful launch starts by agreeing the following items:

- Objectives: How many new customers does the company want to obtain? What sales are expected from day 1? Does the team want to nominate the product or service for an award?

- Budget: How much money is allocated towards the launch to meet the objectives?

- Position: Where in the market is the product or service positioned: expensive or great value, available to all or exclusive?

- Marketing collateral: What is needed: brochures, website, posters, adverts, direct mail, PR?

- Route to market: How is the product being sold: through distributors, direct, online, offline?

- Timetable: How much time is needed for product development, tooling, packaging, product testing, showing to customers and distributors to obtain their reactions?

HINT

Always conduct a client survey to check whether the target group is ready to receive a new product. If they're not ready, the product may need a new target client group or additional work.

See also:

Q33   How will our competitors react?

Q37   How do we win awards?

Q38   How do we protect our idea?

Q80   Should we dump some products?

Q82   How do we survey existing clients?

Q36 How do we generate media attention?

The media are always interested in news. To gain media attention about new products or services, you have to consider what you can share about the product, how it was created, what and who was involved.

Themes for news releases include:

- Awards won by the product, service or company.
- New contracts as a result of the new products.
- Facts and figures, such as how long it took to make, number of widgets used in production, etc.
- Clients' success stories and how the product has helped them.
- The first of its type.
- The only one of its type.
- The largest, smallest, fastest, tallest.
- Unusual applications.
- Most expensive.
- The first time.
- Different.
- Unique.
- Features on individual contributors to the new product development.

Other cost-effective ways to generate media attention include:

- Adding drama to an event.
- Getting local dignitaries to open or sponsor events, as they have their own PR resources.
- Piggy-backing onto larger events that are taking place.

HINT Release news information (including to TV and radio) on 'slow' news days during holidays and when there are no major events taking place. This can be at the start of January, August and December.

See also:

Q64 How do we write press releases?

Q66 Where can we issue news releases online?

Q37   How do we win awards?

Recognition for business success is something that many businesses allow to pass by unnoticed. Entering for an award is a great way of letting all stakeholders know how successful the business is against the performance of its peers.

There are direct benefits for the company too! Winning awards:

- Provides press coverage that you often don't need to organise.
- Marks a difference between you and your competitors.
- Reassures your clients that they've made the right decision.
- Gives credibility in your sector and wider area.
- Makes it easier to recruit and retain staff.

In addition:

- Clients and potential clients notice the success.
- The success can be shared on websites, in newsletters, etc.
- Staff are pleased at the combined success.
- The company's national profile is raised.
- It provides a common goal to work towards.
- It focuses everyone over a time-period.

Ask staff – and suppliers and clients – to pass on details of awards that they are aware of.

HINT

Paperwork for entering awards can be demanding. Set up a document containing everything needed to win an award and selectively pick just one or two awards to start.

If you're not successful in an award, ask for feedback – it's always interesting to see how other people perceive your business. And don't be shy about entering again the next year – provided your 'story' has improved, judges like to see and often reward 'triers'.

See also:

Q32   How do we get the staff involved?

Q38   How do we protect our idea?

There are two key stages to protecting an idea:

- Before the product, service or concept is created: When having initial discussions with third parties, you can ask them to sign a non-disclosure agreement (NDA). These are also known as 'confidentiality agreements' and allow you to keep an idea secret, while sharing it with contacts and suppliers but preventing them from revealing this information to anybody else. NDAs can be used, for example, when you need a supplier to help with an aspect of the product development, whether it's product design, packaging or marketing.

- Before the product, service or concept is made available to the public: Once an idea has been developed, it may need greater legal protection by patent, copyright, design rights. National Patent and Intellectual Property Offices can offer advice and guidance. It may be wise to seek legal advice from a Patent Attorney as patents are territorial and can only be enforced in the areas for which they're granted.

See also:

Q30   How do we research the market?

Q31   How do we value the market and assess demand?

Patent Offices www.patentsoffice.ie and www.ipo.gov.uk

Examples of NDAs www.ipo.gov.uk/patent/info/cda.pdf

Patent Attorneys www.aptma.ie and www.cipa.org.uk

Note – cannot protect an idea – only the
"expression of it"

Q39   How does sponsorship work for smaller businesses?

Smaller business can sponsor many local activities: from local sports clubs to schools. The key issues are to identify something local, with some connection to your business, where you can organise a two-way agreement.

A two-way agreement is more than writing a cheque. It's about getting involved – for example, getting your staff to help at the charity for the day; organising matches between staff and the charity; painting and decorating rooms, as well as staff developing their own skills.

Who can you sponsor?

- Inner city clubs.
- University students.
- Local sports teams.
- Schools.

What can you get in return?

- Research information.
- Your logo being displayed, brand building within an area.
- PR from photos of events.
- News stories for your website and newsletter.
- Opportunities for your staff to work together outside the office.
- Mentoring opportunities for your management team.

Sponsoring a local club does not need to be expensive. €500, along with some time and effort, can make a difference to smaller organisations.

HINT Decide what the company wants to achieve, set a budget and ask staff to nominate potential charities.

See also:

Q32 How do we get the staff involved?

Q40   What is viral marketing?

Viral marketing is a way of getting people to pass on your promotional message so that more people see or hear about your brand. It is often referred to as 'word of mouse'.

In the same way that a cold virus is passed from one person to another, the objective of viral marketing is to hit lots of people at the same time. It is not meant to be malicious, just a cheaper way to promote a brand.

Viral marketing often takes place through an email that one person sends to their friends and so on. The key is creating something of interest that will be passed along the line. Hotmail is often quoted as the best example of viral marketing, as the free email service is seen by and subsequently used by so many people.

A US company making traditional food blenders needed to lift sales and started to film items in their blender. Younger viewers found this very entertaining and started to email clips to each other. This resulted in a dedicated website (www.willitblend.com) showing mobile phones, iPods and golf balls being added to the blender. These videos were added to YouTube (www.youtube.com/user/Blendtec) and shared amongst thousands of people and the sales of the company's blenders increased.

How can we use viral marketing?

The key has to be something useful that people want to 'secretly' share with friends and colleagues. This could be:

- Blog articles on hot or relevant topics.
- The seven secrets of passing certain exams, just before the exam season.
- Eight ways to find a job in a popular sector.
- The three things most businesses should know.

Gimmicks may work, but can be short-lived and there is the danger that they have a negative impact on your brand. Think of viral marketing as part of your marketing toolbox, but use with care.

See also:

Q41   What is buzz marketing?

Q48   How do we create a blog?

Q41   What is buzz marketing?

Buzz marketing is a form of viral marketing and can work offline, as well as online.

Actions are carried out by brand ambassadors or people employed temporarily by a company to create a 'buzz' or stir about their products or services. The idea is to get the media talking positively about your company.

T-Mobile the telephone company released an advert showing people suddenly dancing in the street. The advert was replicated in major UK train stations and other locations. Known as a 'flash mob' the event was posted on Facebook with the instructions "The Trafalgar Square Silent Dance, this is where everyone meets at Trafalgar Square, you play your iPod, or MP3 music player in your ears and dance to your own music. We want to make this the biggest event, so please add all your friends to this group." It created a buzz and was originally thought to be organised by T-Mobile.

Smaller businesses can get friends to act as online brand ambassadors by mentioning their products or services on relevant blogs, endorsing your brands on their MySpace and Facebook profiles or in forums about specific subjects.

Offline buzz marketing may involve people going into a store to ask for a certain product that they know is not available in store, to encourage the store owner to stock the product. The challenge is that this may create artificial demand and no repeat orders will be generated.

HINT   Use buzz marketing with care as, if your tactics are discovered, it can backfire!

See also:

Q40   What is viral marketing?

Q55   How does Facebook work for businesses?

Flash mob events on Facebook

www.facebook.com/event.php?eid=54073341554&ref=nf.

Q42 How does sales promotion work?

Sales promotion is an effort to promote the company's name and create opportunities for sales. It is about:

- Communication: Gaining attention and providing information that may lead the customer to the product.

- Invitation: Direct invitation to purchase now rather than later, through a time-limited offer.

- Incentive: Incorporating a concession, or contribution that gives the customer value for money, such as coupons to collect in return for a discount or premiums.

It can be a 'please' or a 'thank-you'. *Please* can we have the work and / or *thank-you* for the work and your support!

AGA cookers created a sales promotion campaign 'AGA Wanted' with the mission "to track down every AGA in the world to include their owners in our foundry's 300th anniversary celebrations." AGA owners who registered online were emailed by the local store and invited to visit and choose a reward. The email included the additional sales promotion message "there is always a coffee and cake to greet you!"

In the B2B arena, 'pleases' should be small and not too expensive – for example, pens, pencils, notepads, key-rings, fridge magnets, mugs, diaries, folders, bags, etc. B2B 'thank-yous' may be a bottle of champagne at Christmas or chocolates for all staff to celebrate an event.

How do I know what to select?

The first issue is identifying the target client groups and looking at what is useful for them and will enable them to remember the company's name. AGA Cookers offered a 10% discount voucher off their products or a free place at a cookery demonstration.

If you are holding an open day, it is useful to organise sales promotion items for goodie bags.

HINT
Sales promotion items are not accepted in all businesses, especially in the public sector and some large corporations.

See also:

Q55 How does Facebook work for businesses?

Q67 How do we organise open days?

AGA's Facebook page www.facebook.com/event.php?eid=540733 41554&ref=nf#/pages/AGA/48229342711?ref=s.

GROWING
YOUR BUSINESS

This is a new age, where the 10th largest country in the world is Facebook.

Q 43   How can we grow our business?

If your product or service is needed, you can always grow the business by:

- Changing the product offer.
- Changing pricing.
- Developing markets or customers.
- Promoting offers.

Changing the product offer involves:

- Developing new products or services:
- Adding greater value to existing products and services.
- Identifying opportunities for existing clients to sign up for a recurring service.

Changing pricing involves:

- Increasing the average spend or order value per customer.
- Adding / removing / modifying delivery charges / expenses.
- Exploring whether existing clients will buy another service.
- Increasing the order cycle.
- Offering alternatives at different prices online or offline.

Developing markets or customers involves:

- Finding more clients online or offline.
- Segmenting the market and creating different offers for different groups.
- Moving into new markets at home or in other countries.

Promoting offers involves:

- Identifying offers to increase average order value.

Start the process by speaking with clients to identify opportunities. An initial survey will indicate potential and this can be followed up with more in-depth meetings to discuss details.

See also:

Q3   What market research do we need?

Q10   What are the 7 key ways to promote our business?

Q82   How do we survey existing clients?

Q44   How do we segment our business?

Market segmentation means taking the market and dividing it into smaller units, which we call 'segments'. Each group or segment must be different in some way.

A business must analyse the needs and wants of different market segments before determining ITS own niche. This means looking in detail at potential segments and identifying what they really want.

You can segment your market at any time when you suspect there are significant, measurable differences in your market. Look at the different segmentation methods below and identify how your current market operates and what segments you could create.

Segmentation by	What this means
Demographics	Age, gender, income, ethnicity, marital status, education, household size, length of residence, type of residence, profession or occupation.
Psychographics	Personality and emotionally based behaviour linked to purchase choices, attitudes, hobbies, risk aversion, personality and leadership traits, magazines read, TV watched.
Lifestyle	Vacations, hobbies, entertainment, other non-work time pursuits.
Life stages	Chronological benchmarking of people's lives at different ages.
Belief and value systems	Religious, political and cultural beliefs and values.
Geography	Country, region, area, metropolitan or rural location, population density, climate.
Benefit	The use and satisfaction gained by the customer.
Behaviour	The nature and frequency of the purchase, brand loyalty, usage level, benefits sought, reaction to marketing messages.

| HINT | For effective market segmentation, the market must be large enough to justify segmenting because, if the market is small, segmentation may make it smaller, giving segments too small for effective marketing. Measurable differences must exist between segments and the anticipated profits must exceed the additional costs. |

See also:

Q9 How do we find customers?

Q30 How do we research the market?

Q45　　How do we sell our products?

The great thing about products is that they are tangible. Imagine a new printer for your office; you can see photos online, possibly a live demonstration on YouTube, and you can pop into a store to see it working. You can check whether it fits inside your office; whether it makes too much noise; and whether it fits your budget?

The easiest way to sell products is to make something that people want to buy. Selling products depends on the product offering, pricing, route to market, promotion, as well as the people involved and how easy you are to buy from.

Route to market

Think about the route to market, what is it and how can you improve it? Potential routes to market include through:

- A sales team.
- Agents.
- Retail outlets.
- Catalogues or printed media.
- Online.

Price bracket

Larger 'big ticket' goods are often made to order and sold through a dedicated sales team.

Promotion methods

Once the product is ready to sell and the route to market is agreed, you need to decide how to promote the products. It's important to get your message out to your customers before others do.

People

There are often many people involved in the sales process, including your own sales team as well as third parties selling for you. Make sure all those involved are aware of your product offering and how customers can buy.

HINT

When we conduct surveys on behalf of clients, the words we hear most often are "We didn't know they did that". Don't rely on customers using a crystal ball; make sure you tell your customers what you do and keep reminding them.

See also:

Q10   What are the 7 key ways to promote our business?

Q43   How can we grow our business?

Q46   How do we sell our services?

Q46   How do we sell our services?

Services are intangible; clients often don't know what they are getting until it has been delivered. You can't ask an accountant to prepare half your accounts for you to make a decision whether to proceed. It is important to treat services differently because of their special nature.

Selling services	What does this mean to me?
Clients seek and rely on information from personal sources rather than non-personal sources (i.e. adverts).	Who do you know and what can you do with who you know? Seminars are a good way of communicating. Add testimonials, case studies to your websites and in printed materials.
Clients engage in greater information-seeking when buying services rather than products.	Provide potential referees. Provide lots of information online about your business. Create 'factsheets' where relevant.
Clients use physical facilities as a major cue to source quality.	What does your office look like? Think about the physical presentation of any tangible items (reports, letters) and go for the best quality (without appearing wasteful or OTT).
Clients' potential options are smaller with services.	Provide reassurance that buying from you is the right option. Do not refer to competitors, keep the options smaller.
Clients adopt innovations in services more slowly.	Encourage early adoption of the services by highlighting compatibility with other services. Communicate the benefits of your service clearly. Offer trials
Brand-switching is less frequent with services.	Look at the lifetime value of the client; what else can you offer? How can you add more value?

People buy from people and even more so with services. After receiving the service, clients often reflect and wonder whether they've done the right thing. It's important to encourage and measure client delight, so surveys after a service should be a standard process.

See also:

Q16   How do we prepare for client meetings?

Q17   What's in a client proposal?

Q45   How do we sell our products?

Q99   How can we create greater impact meeting new people?

Q47   How do we promote our online store?

Online stores are aimed at those with access to the internet (50% of the adult population in Ireland and 71% in the UK, 2008) and the best way to promote them is online.

Ways to promote your online store include:

- Develop lots of FAQs (Q19).
- Links to your blog (Q20, Q48).
- Promoting your website on other websites (Q50).
- Getting involved with social networking (Q53).
- Identifying opportunities for video that can be uploaded to YouTube (Q56).
- Creating PR (Q36, Q64, Q66).
- Creating podcasts (Q68).
- Looking at opportunities for buzz or viral marketing (Q40, Q41).
- Exploring mobile (SMS) offers (Q91).
- Working on search engine marketing (Q92, Q95).
- Engaging affiliates (Q96).
- Email to a friend.
- Developing useful downloads.
- Showing testimonials from happy customers.
- Organising a chat facility or online help.
- Developing your website so that it can offer personalised recommendations.
- Contributing to other blogs.

If time permits, it is better to create a marketing plan before launching into tactics. A plan gives you *strategic* direction about the products stocked, prices charged and the best promotion tactics for the business. A plan makes you decide which tactics to use from day one. Your budget is agreed, you can get better rates for advertising and no rash decisions are made, as long as you plan.

See also:

Q24 What sales do online businesses generate?

Q26 How do we develop a marketing plan?

Q70 Where can we get marketing help?

UK internet statistics www.statistics.gov.uk/pdfdir/iahi0808.pdf

Ireland internet statistics www.internetworldstats.com/eu/ie.htm

Q48   How do we create a blog?

Creating a blog takes minutes as many blog tools provide ready-made templates and a simple step-by-step approach. Some blog tools are easier to use than others and many are free. To start your blog:

- Select your preferred blog tool: There are many free blog tools including **blogger.com**, **movabletype.org**, **blog.myspace.com**, **wordpress.org** or you can ask your web designer to add a blog to your website.

- Prepare some content: A blog is not a blog without content! In our experience, companies are great at preparing their first and second newsletters, it's the third and later that they struggle with. On this basis, we recommend preparing at least five entries before launching. You should also publish new entries on your blog on a regular(-ish) schedule – you don't have to publish frequently but people are encouraged to check your blog for updates if they expect to find new material there whenever they look.

- Build and maintain your blog: Having selected your blogging tool, choose your preferred template and start adding content. A blog does not need to take up too much time. We aim to post two entries per week and allocate around 10 minutes to do this. Google's **Blogger** has a scheduling facility which means that you can add blog posts several weeks in advance, which is useful if you are going away or expect to be busy at a specific time.

- Promote your blog: Add your blog address to your own website, email signature and list it on your online profiles such as **LinkedIn** (see **Q54**). Register your blog with blog search engines – the best-known is **technorati.com**; others include **blogsearchengine.com**, **google.co.uk/blogsearch** and **zimbio.com**.

> **HINT**
>
> We prepare our blogs in a Word document, so that we can spell-check it, copy and paste and keep a copy on our hard drive, in case the Google Blogger software has a failure and all the content is lost.

See also:

Q20 What is a 'blog'?

Technorati's page about blogs technorati.com/blogging/state-of-the-blogosphere

Quick Win Marketing website www.quickwinmarketing.com for a full list of blog tools and websites

Q49   Why is our website not listed with search engines?

The main search engine is Google, which sells its content to other sites and has become the all-important search engine. There are also specialist search engines that search by industry sector, geographical location.

The main reasons that websites are not listed are:

- The website has not been submitted to search engines (it's blindingly obvious but ...).
- Spiders cannot access the site because it is contained within frames, which are not search engine-friendly.
- The website is database-driven with complex URLs, which are seen as 'less significant'.
- The website has too many pictures and not enough text.
- And conversely, too much text and the keyphrases cannot be seen either.

Google's goal is 'to return highly relevant results for every query' and it works on the basis of a mathematical algorithm that involves over 200 factors. This algorithm changes frequently, so that search engine optimisation companies have to run to stay ahead.

Have a conversation with your web designer and get their opinions about your website!

HINT www.google.co.uk/webmasters contains tools for submitting your website, as well as other useful information on how to get your site listed.

See also:

Q50   How do we get more website traffic?

Q92   What is search engine optimisation?

searchenginewatch.com for a full list of all search engines

Q50   How do we get more website traffic?

Generating traffic flow to a website involves planned activities such as:

- Emailing all customers regularly with an e-newsletter (only those who have opted-in – beware data protection rules).
- Adding a 'visit the website' tagline to all email addresses.
- Registering with directories and search engines.
- Generating links to and from the website.
- Including a 'call to action' to generate sales or enquiries – for example, 'click here to buy gifts', etc.
- Ensuring your contact details are on every page of your website (or a contact us form), ideally situated in the top half of the page.
- Including a 'how to order' page, along with payment options and instructions.
- Most websites are still found via word of mouth – so tell lots of people about the site!
- Try to include some useful items (free stuff) that people can copy or download easily.
- Register with Irish / UK search engines (see **searchenginewatch.com** for hints and tips).

Traffic to your website can be generated by search engines or through other marketing activities you undertake.

So that search engines can see yours is a busy site, the home page should not be static, but should be updated daily, with for example:

- Latest news.
- Poll with topical question.
- Feed from the blog.

- Tips of the month to share with your staff.

A website that has a Content Management System can allow you to prepare the content in advance, going live automatically on the dates you set. This way you do not need to be at your desk every day updating the site.

Other marketing activities include:

- Direct or email campaigns driving traffic to the site.
- Adding useful documents that generate viral or word of mouse visitors.
- Adding your website address to everything, from emails and letters to invoices and handouts.
- Getting connected online through professional networking sites.
- Starting a blog or creating a **Facebook** page.

See also:

Q40   What is viral marketing?

Q48   How do we create a blog?

Q51   How do we revamp our website?

Q55   How does Facebook work for businesses?

www.stardigital.co.uk for PageMasterPRO Content Management System

Q51   How do we revamp our website?

If your website is not getting the visitor numbers you think it deserves, you may need to conduct a review to see how it compares to its competitors.

Bocij developed a 'benefits of an internet presence' framework, based on 6Cs, which you can use to see how your website compares and to see what else you can add or remove from your site:

- Customer service improvement: Ways to make life easier for your clients or customers include adding details of opening hours, maps, information on ordering time, stock availability or customer service questions and podcasts showing 'how to...'. Think about how your website can improve customer service.

- Cost reduction: Look at ways to save money in the office with a better website – for example, reducing telephone calls by providing frequently-needed information such as policies, forms, downloadable marketing material online.

- Competitive advantage: If a company introduces new capabilities before its competitors, then it achieves an advantage until its competitors have the same capability – e.g., photos online for designers; online tracking tools for sales; and booking tools for events companies. What can your business add?

- Communication improvements: All the ways that you can improve communications with customers, staff, suppliers and distributors – for example, online newsletters, RSS feed, internal blogs, and other blogs. How do you communicate with customers?

- Capability: The Internet provides new opportunities for new products and services and for exploiting new markets. Does your website give your business the capability to test the sale of new products?

- Control: Marketing information is available through website visitor reports which show facts and figures. How do you use your data? How else could you use it?

See also:

Q50 How do we get more website traffic?

Q92 What is search engine optimisation?

Q96 What are affiliate schemes?

Q52   How do we get the best out of networking?

Many of us attend networking events, see someone we know and spend the time chatting with them. When we get back to the office, we haven't 'networked' or generated any leads, which is one of the aims of networking.

To get the best out of networking, you need to:

- Prepare: Before attending an event, networking or otherwise, ask yourself a few questions: What do I have to offer other people at the event? Why am I networking? What do I want to achieve? You might want introductions to potential contacts, or to explore opportunities for your own business, to conduct some research or something else. Have a purpose before you go, it's easier to see if you've succeeded and decide whether it's worth attending again.

- Create a first impression: We still judge people on that first meeting, so it's always better to dress up than dress down!

- Say 'Hello': Don't wait for an introduction, introduce yourself, say how your business helps customers. If you see a familiar face, don't wait for someone to remember you, reintroduce yourself, but don't spend too long chatting to one person.

- Focus on quality not quantity: It's not a competition to collect business cards! It's better to speak to three or four people, who will remember you, rather than to collect business cards from everyone in the room, none of whom may remember you at all.

- After the event, stay connected: We meet people at events and then don't speak to them again. You could use LinkedIn to connect and at least you can both see each other's contacts and activities.

> **HINT**
>
> Ask people what sort of customers they are looking for and work at listening to the answer. You may be able to help and this will start to forge a relationship.

See also:

Q54 How do we create **LinkedIn** profiles?

Q99 How can we create greater impact meeting new people?

Q53   What are social networks?

Social networks are websites that enable people to build communities of interest. Most social networks are web-based, which means you do not need any software to get started. Membership is usually free but requires registration, which involves providing socio-demographic information, such as where you live, employment details, education and interests. Social network sites make their money through advertising, some being able tailor adverts to specific users.

The best known social networks are about connecting friends and include **BeBo**, **Facebook**, **MySpace** and **Friends Reunited**. Business networks like **LinkedIn** and **Ecademy** enable users to build contacts, demonstrate their expertise and share information. Head-hunters also use the business networking sites as recruitment tools.

Most sites rely on users to contribute content. Whether it's updates to business profiles or plans for the weekend, these sites would not exist without dialogue between users.

There are challenges with social networks and when something has been published online, it is difficult to remove. There have also been issues with privacy, so some sites like **LinkedIn** enable users to post their first name and last name initial only.

 Check and see how many companies you know are on LinkedIn or other networks. How does it work for them?

See also:

Q54   How do we create **LinkedIn** profiles?

Q55   How does **Facebook** work for businesses?

Q54   How do we create LinkedIn profiles?

LinkedIn is an online network for professionals. It has been described as 'Facebook for business' and started in 2003. A free service, in January 2009 it had over 34 million members in over 200 countries.

Businesses can use LinkedIn for:

- Promoting your expertise and making contacts.
- Finding previous colleagues / connections.
- Researching people.
- Recommending people.
- Browsing other people's connections (as long as they have allowed this in their preferences).
- Promoting your website or blog.
- Searching for people by profession and location.
- Introductions to the millions of members.
- Identifying potential for collaboration.
- Setting up membership or interest groups
- Answering questions and demonstrating credibility.
- Asking questions which can be found by Google.
- Checking out people before you meet them.

There are additional paid-for services, including advertising and poll questions.

Building your LinkedIn Profile

Build your profile by adding your work history, website, blog, your membership groups and awards won. To get started, go to www.linkedin.com and join. This starts to build your profile. It is useful to have your CV to hand, as you will need to enter your current and past positions, as well as details about your education.

A photo can be uploaded at a later stage and you don't need to complete your profile instantly. Your profile can be built by adding contacts, which can be done automatically with your email programme. Making recommendations about people in your contact list also enriches your profile.

Under *Professional Headline* in *Basic Information*, add more than your name and job title, as this line appears every time someone searches for you or sees your name in a contact list.

See also:

Q55   How does **Facebook** work for businesses?

Q55   How does Facebook work for businesses?

Facebook started in 2004 as a social network for college graduates. Today, it claims over 150 million active users and helps people communicate more efficiently with their friends, family and co-workers. It consists of different functions including Profiles, Pages, Events, Groups and Ads.

Historically, Facebook users created groups for their favourite companies. This led Facebook to create Pages so that companies could protect their own brands. Facebook Pages allow businesses to create a free presence on Facebook and build a fan club.

Creating a page for your company will allow 'fans' to find you (registered Facebook users can become a 'fan' of your company):

- Fans can create discussion groups and talk about your products – e.g., the Nokia company page contains photos taken by Nokia fans of their phones and people are talking about them.

- Fans' actions appear on their friends' news feeds so, when someone becomes a fan of a company, their friends will get notified – e.g., (name) has become a fan of (company / person) and this may encourage more visitors to your company page.

- Companies can send news or updates to their fans and can monitor the discussions and check out what people are saying about your company.

- You have direct contact with people who like your products / services – your fans!

- You can add time-limited vouchers or offers onto the page.

Profiles are for individuals to add their personal details. Having a profile enables a company to create a page.

Events can be added to the Facebook calendar and users are invited to join or support the event. Events can be used for fund-raising, parties, good causes, political statements, education and meetings.

Groups can be for business, entertainment, common interest, geography, internet, just for fun, music, sports, students and organisations. Groups can be open to anyone who wants to join or they can be restricted in some way.

Facebook Ads allows businesses to create targeted ads aimed at the target audience. The message can be targeted to users based on age, geography, interests, relationship status, education and other variables.

See also:

www.facebook.com

Q56 How can we use YouTube?

YouTube is an online video website and lets people and businesses watch and share original videos worldwide. Once you have opened a free account, YouTube allows you to upload and share video clips on www.YouTube.com and across the Internet through websites, mobile devices, blogs, and email. Video gives companies greater control and enables your side of the story to be seen and created.

The cost of video has dropped with new mini video recorders such as the **Flip Digital Camcorder**, which is less than £100. The Flip has a USB connection, which means you can plug it straight into your PC without any complex software. Traditionally, a film crew for one day costs from €2,000 to €3,000 and this would generate two to four news items. Smaller camcorders have reduced quality, but this is seen as acceptable for YouTube.

Users can decide whether to share a video amongst the world, or only select users. This can be helpful for companies sharing meeting information, interviewing job candidates or for training purposes.

The site also allows users to insert a YouTube video into **Facebook** and **MySpace** accounts, blogs, or other Web sites where anyone can watch them.

Your company can use video to add clips to its website. These can also be posted to YouTube. Clips you could add include:

- Show how products are made.
- Show your customer service team in action.
- Show how products work.
- Introduce staff.
- Highlight product quality.

See also:

Q40   What is viral marketing?

www.theflip.com/products_flip_ultra.shtml

Q57   What is bluecasting?

Bluecasting is bluetooth broadcasting, using short-range wireless systems to send messages to mobile phones near a specific location. It is also called 'proximity marketing'.

Bluecasting involves setting up broadcasting equipment at a given location – typically a store, shopping centre or train station – and then sending information such as text, images, audio or video to a bluetooth-enabled device, such as mobile phone, PDA or laptop.

Bluecasting depends on devices being set up to receive these messages. In the past, many users would ensure their mobile phones were set to 'hidden' or 'off' mode to avoid receiving messages. To counter this, bluecasting became more creative and offered something valuable to the mobile phone user, such as ringtones, discounts, previews or video clips, encouraging the user to share their details.

Bluecasting is more useful for customers in retail or business to consumer environments. These companies can use bluecasting to:

- Promote offers in certain locations.
- Create a customer database or mailing list.
- Encourage spending in slow times.

See also:

Q40   What is viral marketing?

Q91   What is interactive marketing?

Q58   How do we write a mailshot?

It is essential to stay in touch with existing clients. Mailshots are different from 'eshots' and are a good way of keeping your name in front of your clients. As a client relationship develops, there is a good chance it becomes less formal. This means that potential competitors can contact your clients, send them information and ensure their identity is on your client's desk.

To counter this, it is essential to maintain visible contact. Informal communications such as emails and telephone calls are great, but they are 'invisible'. Letters and newsletters have a greater presence and can be passed to other people in the organisation.

Direct mail has four crucial steps:
1. Introduction.
2. Detail.
3. Offer or close, ideally time-limited.
4. Instruction or call to action: most people don't know what action to take when they've received a letter.

To start your campaign:
- Add the letters as a task to your diary system.
- Agree who is sending out the letters.
- Complete the letters.
- Prepare the lists (i.e., who the letters are being sent to).
- Schedule the mailings.

HINT During a downturn, fewer mailings are sent! It's the best time to start a campaign, as potential customers may be looking at ways to get greater value and may be in the mood to switch suppliers.

See also:

Q59 What should we include in newsletters?

Q60 Where can we buy mailing lists?

Q61 How many mailings should we send out?

Q62 How do we organise an email campaign?

Q59   What should we include in newsletters?

To ensure newsletters sent to clients are read, they need to include newsworthy and useful items.

Newsletters can be one sheet of A4 printed both sides or a folded A3 page printed on all four sides. Contents can include:

- News and updates.
- Hints and tips.
- Case studies to demonstrate the company's expertise.
- Quotes from happy clients that act as mini-testimonials.
- Industry facts and figures.
- Staff profiles to build rapport with your readers.

How else can we use newsletters?

- When prepared, they can be printed as a PDF and added to your website for visitors to download.
- Email them to contacts.
- Convert them to a podcast and upload them to your websites.

How often should we issue newsletters?

It depends on the content available. If there is plenty of content, a newsletter could be issued monthly. More than this can be too much for clients. A quarterly or term-time only newsletter often can give a regular update without being too intrusive.

HINT

The greatest challenge with newsletters is generating content. In your enthusiasm to make the first newsletter really good, there is a danger of including too much in it – leaving you with nothing for later newsletters. Encourage staff to contribute stories and have monthly newsletter meetings or lunches to generate content.

A veterinary practice we know issues four newsletters a year promoting topical events such as 'pet passports' towards holiday season, suggestions for Christmas gifts and updates on vaccinations at other times. Staff are encouraged to add content and often feature in the newsletter with their own pets and recent events they have held.

Budget Tip

If posting less than 100 A4 regular newsletters, it is more cost-effective to organise pre-printed newsletter paper and simply print off via a colour printer. This means you can personalise some stories for specific groups or individuals.

See also:

Q68 How do we podcast?

Q60   Where can we buy mailing lists?

Mailing lists are built from various sources. List brokers buy lists from some membership associations, or magazine subscription details and when shoppers complete warranty cards. Some list brokers are also 'list compilers' and create their own lists by telephoning organisations or companies and obtaining contact details and other information.

Reputable list brokers are likely to be members of a Direct Marketing Association who abide by Codes of Practice and have significant experience.

Consumer lists may be broken down by geography, purchasing behaviour or life stages, such as large and small families, older people or those starting out on their own.

Business lists may come from a central directory, such as **Kompass**, and may include further development where the broker contacts the company to ask more questions and gathers information about the company's future plans.

Both consumers and businesses can opt-out of receiving marketing information, so any list you buy should be checked against this. Equally, when you send out information, give the recipient the chance to opt-out of any future contact.

Most list brokers will tell you how and when the information was collected. They will also provide the list in the format that best suits your database. Check the broker's policy for returned 'gone away' mail.

When you buy a mailing list, it may be:

- Single-use basis: you can use it only once and must not use again without permission. Lists may include spoof names, so the broker will be able to tell if you misuse their data.

- Multi-use: the contract will state how many times or for how long you can use the data, which is usually within a 12 month period.

- Outright purchase: this is where you buy the list with no restrictions and have unlimited usage.

See also:

Irish Direct Marketing Association www.idma.ie

Direct Marketing Association UK www.dma.org.uk

List brokers include **www.dataireland.ie** and **www.bill-moss.com**

www.dma.org.uk/Supplier/lst-Glossary.asp useful glossary of list buying terms

Q61   How many mailings should we send out?

Mailshots or mailings are useful in business to business (B2B) environments. A business to consumer (B2C) company may opt for advertising, depending on the total number of people to be mailed.

B2B may send mailings weekly, monthly, quarterly or timed to link to another event. The number of mailings sent depends on the target customer group. We receive weekly flyers from our stationery suppliers but we usually order once a month. As we receive what we feel is too many mailings, they are now recycled and not read at all. These mailings are also intended for everyone rather than focusing on the key products we regularly buy. It would be better for the supplier to send fewer, but more targeted mailings.

Finding a balance depends on your product offering and how often purchases are made. The balance for a professional service that is only purchased once a year is probably two targeted letters. Sent to the right people, these letters are likely to be retained until the service is needed.

In an ideal world, your company plans all its marketing activities at the start of the financial or calendar year, deciding the most relevant times to contact clients or customers. The plan may look like this:

	Existing customers	Potential customers: Group 1	Potential customers: Group 2
Jan / Feb	New Year update		
Mar / Apr		Invite to workshop	
May / Jun	Update		New product launch info
Jul / Aug			
Sep/ Oct		Update and intro to new staff	
Nov / Dec	Christmas cards		Invite to exhibition

In the B2C environment, mailings may be monthly or every two months, focusing on specific offers. It is essential to make any offer time limited – i.e., state when the offer starts and stops. If not, years later, a potential customer will find the offer!

HINT
If your business has a slow day and you have organised your plan for the year, it's a good time to print off newsletters, ready to send on the agreed date. Planning in advance means less panic!

See also:

Q60 Where can we buy mailing lists?

Q62   How do we organise an email campaign?

You need a list where people have opted-in to receive your mailings. Ideally an email campaign should take place in stages as shown in the following table. The critical factor is not to send out too many emails in one go, as sending emails in smaller blocks of 10 and 20 will make any follow-up easier.

Overleaf is an example of an email campaign plan:

Message Type	1. Introduction	2.Detail	3. Visit now
Interval / Trigger Condition	Look at us and visit the site.	1 month: inactive (i.e. have not visited site).	1 month: inactive.
Outcomes Required	Click through to site. Increase awareness of brand.	Click through to site.	Click through to site.
Email Subject	Batty gifts for Christmas.	Only 45 shopping days left before Christmas.	Last orders for bat gifts before Christmas.
Content	We have a range of wonderful gifts for the batty people in your life. Bat detectors, super torches and lots of books. Click here (link to landing page) to see the full Christmas list or free factsheets.	Still trying to find that perfect gift? Buying from the Bat Company gives you perfect gifts and helps bat conservation too. Orders placed today will still arrive before Christmas. There's even time to get the present gift wrapped. Click here (link to landing page with testimonials) and see what other people are already saying about useful bat gifts.	All orders placed today will arrive before Christmas. The Bat Company works on bat conservation and needs your help. Books from €5, educational tapes and bat detectors to listen to bats in your garden. For interesting and thoughtful gifts click here.

See also:

Q12 How do we create a mailing list?

Q60 Where can we buy mailing lists?

Annmarie
I had to turn table to get it to fit – even then had to go to next page! OK??
B

Q63 How can we monitor our competitors?

Keeping a close eye on competitors is useful and is part of the marketing process. It is useful for:

- Exploring whether prices are changing in the market.
- Unravelling competitors' range of products and services.
- Identifying whether new opportunities are available for your business.
- Gaining an early warning if there are threats on the horizon.

Ways to monitor competitors

- Engage a cuttings service.
- Sign up for free Google Alerts.
- Conduct mystery shopping.
- If the company is listed on the stock exchange, buy a few shares and you will receive newsletters, mailshots and plenty of shareholder information about the company's future plans and past performance.
- Sign up for newsletters on the competitors' websites where offered.

When the information has been gathered, make sure that all relevant staff are aware. A short summary near the kettle is a good place to share news.

 HINT Nominate one person to be responsible for collating and sharing the information on competitors.

See also:

Q34 What are Google Alerts?

Q65 What is a cuttings service?

Q81 How does mystery shopping work?

Q64   How do we write press releases?

Traditionally, press releases were physically posted to newspapers. Today, they are usually emailed, which makes it easier for journalists to 'copy and paste'.

When writing a press release, start with the content:

- Say who you are.
- Explain what you have done.
- Give some details about where this took place, as this gives the 'local interest' angle.
- Describe why, when and how?

In terms of style of a press release:

- Keep it short: one page if possible, as you can always provide more information if needed.
- The title should be simple and clear, indicating what is to follow.
- Put all the main information and key points in the first paragraph.
- Each paragraph should work on its own.
- The main body of the text should expand on the key points emphasised in the first paragraph.
- Keep sentences simple and short.
- Avoid jargon and technical language.
- Try and give examples relevant to the audience.
- At the end of the press release, make sure you include your contact details.

HINT Submitting a photo with the press release increases its chances of getting published.

See also:

Q65 What is a cuttings service?

Q66 Where can we issue news releases online?

Q65   What is a cuttings service?

Cuttings, press or media monitoring agencies offer a service that scans selected newspapers or magazines looking for stories based on their clients' needs. They started as companies were missing stories about themselves that featured in the press, but it was not practical to buy every paper every day and read each page. Many large companies use these services.

Most countries have companies offering this service. Historically, it was difficult to obtain local newspapers in other countries, added to which, there were potential language barriers. It was also usual for cuttings services to physically cut out the news story or article, stick it onto a page and post it to the client. Today, the internet contains local and national stories that are available at the click of a mouse. As the number of online publications grows, you can receive the latest news direct to your in-box.

Traditionally, a cuttings service costs €200 per month plus a 'per clip' charge, which varies around €5 for each magazine article and €2 for each newspaper cutting. The best known names in the business are **Durrant** and **Romeike**.

Newer lower cost alternatives to the traditional service have started to appear. They offer an internet-based, rather than paper-based, service. These services charge a monthly fee, no additional 'per clip' charges and can be switched on and off as needed. Some offer free trials for one or two weeks – for example:

- **Newsnow** (www.newsnow.co.uk/services/presscuttings) monitors your chosen papers in the UK and internationally.

- Dublin-based **Zenark** (www.zenark.com) offers an online search engine that monitors Irish press and all Government departments' websites.

- **www.cyberalert.com** provides an international electronic cuttings service.

> **HINT**
>
> It is still possible that cuttings will be missed! If you know something is appearing in a local or specialist publication, subscribe to it directly and monitor it internally.

See also:

Q34 What are Google Alerts?

www.durrants.co.uk

www.uk.cision.com

Q66   Where can we issue news releases online?

In addition to the usual printed media, there are many opportunities to 'post' news releases online. Some sites seek entire articles and others are looking for latest news. Most require registration before you can start submitting press releases.

Website	Details
www.prlog.org/ie	PRLog is a free online press release service with a dedicated space for Irish stories.
www.irishpressreleases.ie	Irish Press Releases offers free online press release services to Irish companies.
www.pressreleasepoint.com/ireland	Free press release distribution website.
www.clickpress.com	ClickPress is a provider of free tools and websites to media professionals around the world.
www.ukprwire.com	Part of ClickPress, with a UK focus.
www.ezinearticles.com	EzineArticles.com where writers can post their articles to be featured in the site.
www.articlealley.com	Articlealley is a free article directory, built in 2004 to help authors promote and syndicate their content.

Submitting press releases online is a great way for a business to mention key words so search engines pick it up. To see if the articles are mentioned, use Google Alerts.

HINT | Most free online PR websites offer free tips and advice about submitting press releases.

See also:

Q34 What are Google Alerts?

Q67   How do we organise open days?

Open days are opportunities for:

- Clients and staff to meet.
- Clients to see where the company is based.
- Clients to better understand how the office works.
- To re-frame a perception about the company being small.

Open days could also provide an opportunity to educate customers about changes in legislation, new products or services as well as being a 'thank you'.

The best times for holding an open day are over a lunchtime or late afternoon. Some refreshments should be provided along with a 'goodie bag', which may include company literature or sales promotion items.

What's involved?

- Identify the clients to invite.
- Prepare the running order (welcome, tour of the building, speakers, drinks, lunch, exit and gift).
- Organise the support material (caterers, gifts, photographer, etc).
- Issue invitations.
- Prepare goodie bags.
- Prepare the room(s) for the event.

HINT

If you don't have a big enough office or building to hold an open day, you could use a local golf course, sports venue, museum (especially outside peak season) or contact An Taisce (www.antaisce.org) about staging an event at one of its venues. If you sponsor a local club, perhaps you could use their venue?

See also:

Q39 How does sponsorship work for smaller businesses?

Q42 How does sales promotion work?

Q68   How do we podcast?

A podcast is an audio file, usually an MP3 file, that you can download from a website. A vodcast is a video file. The idea is that your clients or customers can subscribe online and, once they have subscribed, the latest episodes will be sent to their desktop or mobile phone.

Companies are starting to use podcasts instead of printed words to keep clients up-to-date, and instead of music when holding for someone on the telephone, to explain something complicated. We believe Google is now searching by sound as well as text, which will make podcasts more important.

The steps involved in a podcast are:

- Record and edit something: You need recording and editing software, which is available free as Open Source – for example, editing software audacity.sourceforge.net or you can buy ready-made software at **www.podproducer.net/en/index.html**. You also need a minidisc recorder and microphone (if recording in the field) or you can use a Skype headset.

- Edit the recording: Once you have edited your recording, you will need to save it as an MP3 file, which makes the file smaller and easier for others to download and listen to. See **iTunes** www.apple.com/itunes or **LAME** audacity.sourceforge.net/help/faq?s=install&item=lame-mp3.

- Publish it on the internet: Upload your recording to your blog. If you don't have a blog or webspace, you can publish your podcast on various sites such as **OurMedia** (free) (www.ourmedia.org). **Juice** is a useful resource with many links (juicereceiver.sourceforge.net). See also **www.podcastalley.com/add_a_podcast.php**.

- Create a subscription feed: Once you have uploaded your recording, you will need to create a feed. A feed allows listeners to subscribe to your products – for example, **www.feedburner.com**.

HINT Record several podcast episodes at the same time, as this ensures you have ongoing content ready to upload.

See also:

ukpodcasters.org.uk

www.podireland.org

www.podcastpickle.com

Q69   How do we get staff uniforms on a budget?

Staff uniforms in the traditional sense are an emotive subject. Some people love them, as they don't need to think about what to wear to work; others hate the rigidity they can bring.

Smaller companies often cannot afford the costs of designing and creating uniforms from scratch. Instead, you can adopt a different approach:

- Look at the business's brand colours and agree the preferred colours that people are happy to wear to the office.
- Ask a couple of staff to visit department stores and see if they have jackets, trousers and skirts in those colours.
- Ask the store to put a selection of items to one side.
- Make a list of all staff who require branded clothes.
- List their preferred sizes.
- Either give staff time off to visit the store and buy the clothing or appoint a couple of staff to make the purchases. If you are buying from well-known department stores, you should be able to take the clothes back, if the sizes are incorrect.
- Local embroidery companies can embellish jackets, shirts and sweaters, by adding a company logo.

You can remove the rigidity of a uniform by giving staff a choice of jackets, trousers, skirts from a particular range, which is where department stores' own-label items offer a good selection.

The **National Trust** (www.nationaltrust.org.uk) engages many volunteers to act as guides to historic buildings in England, Wales and Northern Ireland. Uniforms for so many people would be expensive and could be seen as not the best use of money raised. Instead, volunteers wear a pin badge to distinguish 'staff' from visitors.

Sometimes, it's only a couple of reception staff who really need a uniform. A uniform worn by reception staff has the instant impact of making a smaller company look bigger, more co-ordinated and more impressive. Uniforms are also great for open days.

See also:

Q23 What is ambient marketing?

Q67 How do we organise open days?

Q70   Where can we get marketing help?

Marketing help is available from many sources, both public and private sector. Many professional bodies include membership directories where you can search for professional help – for example:

Organisation	Website	Details
Business Links	www.businesslink.gov.uk	A UK free business advice and support service, available online and through local advisers.
Chartered Institute of Marketing	www.cim.co.uk	International body for marketing and business development, with a directory of marketing consultants.
Chartered Society of Designers	www.csd.org.uk	The professional body for designers with over 3000 members in 34 countries
County & City Enterprise Boards	www.enterpriseboards.ie	Enterprise Boards support the start-up and development of local business in Ireland. Support includes advice, mentoring and grants or financial support for training and growth.
Design Business Association	www.dba.org.uk	The trade association for the UK design industry.
Institute of Designers in Ireland	www.idi-design.ie	Professional body representing the interests of Irish designers. Its function is to promote high standards of design.

Organisation	Website	Details
Irish Internet Association	www.iia.ie	The professional body for those conducting business via the internet from Ireland.
Marketing Institute of Ireland	www.mii.ie	The Marketing Institute of Ireland is the professional body for marketing people, with a directory of marketing consultants and services.
PLATO	www.plato.ie	Ireland's most successful SME development organisation dealing exclusively with owner-managed businesses. Over the past 10 years, more than 2,000 owner-managers have participated in the PLATO programme in Ireland and have experienced the benefits to their business.
UK Web Design Association	www.ukwda.org	Aims to encourage and promote industry standards within the British web design and new media sector.

HINT

If you're on a budget, the business schools within universities often have marketing students seeking placements where they can obtain practical marketing experience.

Q71   How do we manage a sales plan to ensure that we achieve our targets?

Once you have created a sales plan, the next stage is to make sure it happens. A sale is a journey and goes through various stages. This journey is often called the 'sales cycle', which is about the time and processes between the initial customer contact to when payment is received.

The length of a sales cycle depends on the company, type of business, the sales team, the market and the customer need. In a retail situation, the sales cycle can be minutes as customers enter the store, see what they need and make the purchase. For larger business to business purchases, the cycle can take months or years. Managing the sales plan involves an understanding of the sales cycle.

From the client's perspective, key stages involved in a sale are:

- Identifying the problem to be solved.
- Seeking potential solutions.
- Requesting information.
- Considering alternatives.
- Evaluating the options.
- Making a decision.
- Placing the order.

Identify all those involved in delivering the sales plan and ensure they understand what is expected of them. To keep on top of the plan, it is a good idea to meet regularly, ideally weekly, to understand where a sale is in the cycle. Ask the sales team to highlight all sales over a certain value and to share with the team where the sale is. If there are blockages and a sale is stuck at a certain point, get others to contribute and generate ideas to progress the sale.

Some sales people are better at 'continuing' rather than 'progressing' a sale. This is because they are stuck or enjoy chatting with clients. In these cases, taking another salesperson to a meeting can move the sale along.

> **HINT**
>
> Sometimes a sale will get stuck due to external factors – when it does, it's often better to walk away and ask the potential customer to call again when they're ready.

See also:

Q13 How do we set sales targets?

Q14 How do we work out the sales leads needed to achieve our sales targets?

Q15 What's in a sales plan?

REVITALISING
YOUR BUSINESS

It costs five times more to acquire a new customer than to retain an existing one.
Phillip E Pfeifer

Q72   How do we revitalise our business?

Determine first why the business is in decline or why products or services have been abandoned. This could be due to resource constraints, poor management or because the company and its products / services are of limited value to the customer.

The next step is to examine whether the world you operate in will support a revitalisation strategy. Are there any changing fashions that could re-launch a specific element of the business?

Also consider what the product or company name means to customers and whether this is positive or negative. Is it time for a change? There may be an opportunity to reinvent the business and change focus.

Traditional customers may have gone, but is there a potential segment to be reached such as an opportunity in an area where competitors are weak? How else can the business offer better value for customers? Sometimes, you may need to move towards a different customer group and 'fire' existing customers. Getting your team together and developing a 'SWOT filter' is a good place to start.

HINT Customer surveys are a great way to find out why a business has lost its way.

See also:

Q74   How can we use a SWOT filter?

Q77   How do we fire customers?

Q82   How do we survey existing clients?

Q83   How do we survey lapsed clients?

Q84   How do we survey potential clients?

Q73   Do we need a brand map?

A brand is a promise and a brand map provides a summary of that promise. It is a useful tool when:

- Recruiting staff.
- Deciding what marketing actions to take.
- Considering potential partnership or other opportunities.

It is a checklist that the business can use to ensure that business decisions fit within the brand map. It consists of five key elements.

Brand Products and Services

- What are the services and products offered? Make a list of what's available now.
- When considering new products and services, check that they fit with the existing mix.

Brand Image

- What image do your clients, customers, shareholders have of the business?
- How do you know this? If you're unsure of the brand image, conduct a survey.

Brand Values

- What does your organisation stand for or represent? Or what's important to the organisation?
- When recruiting new staff, find out what's important to them and assess whether it matches your values.

Brand Personality

- How would you describe the personality of the brand?
- Do potential partners match this personality?

- Do new products and services fit with the existing brand personality?

Brand Uniqueness

- What is unique about your offer?
- Do new products and services add or detract from this uniqueness?

Get your staff involved, as they may have different opinions about the company's image, personality and values.

See also:

Q32   How do we get the staff involved?

Q82   How do we survey existing clients?

Q84   How do we survey potential clients?

Q74   How can we use a SWOT filter?

A SWOT analysis is a simple list of the company's Strengths, Weaknesses, Opportunities and Threats (SWOT). It is a useful starting point to assess where work may be needed.

A SWOT filter takes the SWOT analysis to the next stage and makes it easier to work on. The filter shows how strengths will be defended, action needed on weaknesses and how to prioritise opportunities and threats.

Strengths are inside the business and are areas where it is performing well. List the business's strengths and how these will be defended, like this:

Strengths	Defensive Action	
	Medium-term	Short-term
Great sales team	Ensure they remain motivated.	Say 'thank you'.

Weaknesses are inside the business, which has the ability to change these issues. List the business's weaknesses and the magnitude of these items and action to remove or reduce them, like this:

Weaknesses	Magnitude		
	Small	Large	Very Large
Weak sales team			Need to organise a sales plan, engage the team and decide the next steps.

Threats are outside the control of the business and are future dangers that may have a negative impact. Threats may occur as a result of new legislation, political, environmental, social, technological, economic or demographic changes. List threats that would have an impact on your business. Then score the probability of occurrence within the next 12 months – 10 points if very likely and 1 if not likely. Finally, rate the seriousness of the threat. Seriousness may be measured by the market declining, or business units having to close or being re-modelled. Use the same 1 to 10 scale. Look at the threats with the highest scores and decide what action is needed to protect the business from them.

Threats	Probability of Occurrence	Seriousness

See also:

Q28   How do we identify opportunities?

Q29   How do we decide which opportunities will work?

Q75   How can we generate more business from existing customers?

More business can be generated from existing customers by increasing the usage rate or through product modification.

Encourage more frequent use

This involves identifying ways for customers to use the product or service more frequently – for example:

- *Kellogg's Cornflakes* encouraging people to eat cereal for supper or as a snack.

- Dentists booking appointments with dental hygienists to scale and polish teeth.

- Accountants providing bookkeeping services or regular review meetings.

More usage per occasion

Where a customer would use one product, encourage them to use two – for example, shampoo manufacturers encouraging people to have two rinses per wash.

New and more varied uses

Customers can be educated in alternative uses of existing products – for example:

- Recipes on food labels to encourage other uses and repeat purchases.

- Podcasts can be created and added to the company's website, added to the telephone system for customers on hold and / or emailed to customers.

Product modification is another way to stimulate sales by adapting quality, features or style.

Quality improvement

Increase the product's functional performance: durability, reliability, taste, etc. This relies on the customer accepting that product is 'new and improved' and being happy to pay for higher quality.

Feature improvement

Add new features to enhance versatility. This shows that you are an innovative company and may spin-off news-worthy press releases. It's worth noting that features may be imitated by competitors, so benefits here could be short-term.

Style improvement

Enhance the aesthetic appeal of the product, which helps develop a unique market identity and may help develop a cult status – for example, the iMac computer is functional but, more importantly, is fashionable.

The effects of style strategy are difficult to predict: Who will like the new style? Will existing customers like it, or will they abandon the product?

See also:

Q86   How do focus groups work?

Q76   How can we find new customers?

New customers may be found online and offline. Online, there are tender websites including:

- ted.europa.eu.
- www.e-tenders.gov.ie.
- www.supply2.gov.uk.
- etenders.london2012.com, the site for the UK Olympics.

Offline, the aims are to:

- Convert non-users.
- Enter new market segments.
- Win competitors' customers.

Convert non-users

Recruit customers who do not use the product or service – e.g., special offers to encourage potential customers to 'have a go'.

Enter new market segments

Enter geographic or demographic areas that use the product but not the brand – e.g., Johnson & Johnson promoting baby shampoo to adult users.

Win competitors' customers

Encourage non-users to switch brand – e.g., during a downturn, if your company offers better value than a major firm, this is a good time to encourage their customers to switch to you.

See also:

Q26   How do we develop a marketing plan?

Q70   Where can we get marketing help?

Q78   How can we find new markets?

Q77   How do we fire customers?

Sometimes, you need to 'fire' or 'sack' a customer. Some customers take too long to pay bills; they pay a lower rate due to historical reasons; they are never happy with the service they receive or your company can no longer accommodate their needs. You may be better off without them!

However, on occasion, even though you might wish otherwise, you have to retain a customer because they are strategically important to the business or they are well-known and have greater external influences. But, if losing the customer will not have a negative impact on your business, it is safe to fire them.

Wait until you receive the next order from them and:

- Advise the customer that they will need to pay in advance, as your company can no longer support their late payments; or

- Thank the customer for the order and say that you have reviewed all pricing and there will be an increase to the order; or

- Ask them to pay early and pay more!

The customer then has the choice to take their business elsewhere or pay earlier or more.

HINT   Make sure all staff are aware of your plans before you take action.

Q78   How can we find new markets?

New markets may be on your doorstep or further away. To find new markets:

- Conduct a survey with existing clients to understand their future plans.
- Conduct market research to identify future trends.
- Get staff to help identify opportunities.

New markets may be a segment of your existing market or based on newer customers from a different location.

Launching a new product or service is another way to find new markets.

Use this checklist for entering a new market:

Area to check	My answer
Potential market size?	
Potential market value?	
Is the market accessible?	
Is it a crowded market or is there room to grow?	
Is the product desired and acceptable?	
Do I have a significantly different offer?	
Is it politically viable / stable?	
What is the cost of entry?	
How long before I get my investment back?	

See also:

Q28   How do we identify opportunities?

Q29   How do we decide which opportunities will work?

Q30   How do we research the market?

Q35   How do we launch new products or services?

Q44   How do we segment our business?

Q82   How do we survey existing clients?

Q79   How can we win more pitches?

A pitch can be a letter, proposal, presentation, or a 50-page tender document. Before you start typing, check that a pitch is needed and ask yourself some questions.

Have I met or do I know this company?

If I don't know you, I'm really not likely to buy from you. If it's a commodity, I might just negotiate with my usual supplier. If it's something else, it's about hearts and minds. How can you win me over if we haven't met?

Do they have the funds to pay for the product or service?

If they don't have the money and you're not a charity, stop right there!

You can test that you're in the right ballpark by verbally indicating the costs involved: 'To deliver this service usually costs between €2,000 and €3,500, how does this sound to you?'. If they say 'expensive', you need to ask compared to what? Test their finances by asking, 'Is that the sort of number you have in your budget?'.

Rehearse the proposal

Before starting the proposal document, when you are sitting in front of the client, talk your way through the pitch or proposal with the client and ask, 'What happens next?'. For example: 'Just imagine that I will organise a visit to identify all the work needed to deliver this service. I will list all the steps to be taken in some detail. Then I will highlight the travel expenses, the fees and the optimum dates for the work to be done and spend several hours putting this into a proposal for you and then present this to your team, demonstrating that this will meet your requirements. I can put all this in writing, but what would happen next?'

Your potential clients may say, 'I'll show it to the board', to which you should respond, 'Perhaps we can both save time and I could meet them and go through the issues?'. If they say that they need to think it over, ask what is it they need to think about.

Get commitment before starting the proposal

You can 'test' the prospect and ask negative questions:

- It sounds like you're not really keen on doing this?
- It sounds like you're trying to benchmark your existing provider?
- It sounds like you're exploring (marketing, IT, websites, haulage) but is it really on the agenda for this year?

HINT	
	Don't be afraid to walk away!

Q80   Should we dump some products?

Sometimes, a product has reached the end of its 'shelf-life'. There are many theories about Product Life Cycle, which works for both products and services.

Before dumping a product, it is essential to conduct some research. This can highlight potential opportunities and give the company a clear focus to move forward.

Area to explore	Questions to ask
Determine why the product has been abandoned or is in decline.	Is this due to resource constraints? Could we sell the product to another company that has more resources? Could we raise more resources? Is this due to poor management? Will training help? Does the product have limited value to the customer? Contact them to find out
Examine whether the external environment will support a rejuvenation strategy.	Look outside the business: Are there any changing fashions that could re-launch a specific item?
What does the product or company name mean to customers?	Conduct a survey: Is the opinion positive or negative? Do customers feel that it's time for a change? Are there other opportunities? Can the company reinvent itself to the customer group or change focus?
Is there a potential segment to be reached?	Look at competitor research and see whether it highlights gaps that could be filled.

Area to explore	Questions to ask
Better value for customers.	Are there opportunities to create better value for customers such as moving offshore, removing part of the product or service, or producing a lower cost version?

See also:

Q30   How do we research the market?

Q84   How do we survey potential clients?

Q81   How does mystery shopping work?

To check whether your own business is working well, it is useful to get someone not known to the staff to visit, telephone or make an online enquiry. The aim is to check the service, product range and to compare the results to similar companies. You need to allocate a budget to buy a few items.

In all cases, you need to create a scenario and visit the shop or telephone the office or go online. A scenario may be 'I'm looking for an outfit for a certain event' or 'My company wishes to buy 100 of these products and I need more information about your quality standards'. When your scenario is ready, make a list of the stores to visit or companies to contact, including competitors.

For retail stores:

- Note the date and time of your visit.
- Note the shops either side: what do they sell and describe the impression given by their windows.
- Describe the inside of the shop: is it easy to see the products and easy to buy?
- If changing rooms are available say what these are like: good mirrors, lighting, space to hang clothes?
- Who is inside the store? Describe the customers and staff.
- What does the shop do well?
- And not so well?

For online shops:

- Look through the website and email them with your scenario.
- Note how long it takes them to respond and the type of response received.
- After the response, make a purchase.

- How long does it take for the goods to arrive?
- How are the items presented?

For business to business:

- Telephone and assess the response.
- How many people do you need to speak to before you get a response?
- Do they offer a brochure or other information?

Budget Tip

Find a business buddy, someone you know and trust, in a non-competing business and gather competitor information for each other.

See also:

Q51   How do we revamp our website? (The answer includes a framework to objectively assess websites.)

Q63   How can we monitor our competitors?

Q82   How do we survey existing clients?

A business to business client survey is best conducted via telephone. People are too busy to write everything down and return surveys by post. Online surveys can work if they are very short, but we have found telephone surveys quite effective. Typically, we generate a 28% response rate. The remainder of those called are often out of the office, on holiday, in meetings. Only a small number decline to participate.

The best surveys are short and to the point. We have found that these questions provide feedback on why a company is popular or not, details about the competition and opportunities for new products.

Questions for active clients:

- Why did you select our company?
- What do you use our company for?
- Do you use any other company for these services or products?
- What do you like about our company?
- What do you dislike about our company?
- What change is likely to have a benefit on your company (other than pricing)?
- What kind of added value are you looking for?
- How can we help improve your product or process?
- What can we do to add value to your process?
- Have your purchases stayed the same, decreased or increased in the last 12 months?
- Has your budget for next year been increased, stayed the same or been decreased for next year?
- Any other comments or is there anything I've missed?

> **HINT**
> Write to all clients when the survey has been concluded and thank them for their help, explain what the business has learnt and tell them what will happen next.

See also:

Q75 How can we generate more business from existing customers?
Q83 How do we survey lapsed clients?

Q83 How do we survey lapsed clients?

Lapsed clients are those who bought from you once upon a time but, for some reason, have started shopping somewhere else. We often ignore lapsed clients as we're a bit embarrassed to speak to them.

The best approach is to ask a third party to conduct the survey as the customer will be more honest and will not hurt your feelings!

Questions to ask lapsed clients:

- Why did you originally select our company?
- What did you mainly use our company for?
- Do you currently use any other company for these services or products?
- Why did you switch from our company?
- Are there any factors that are likely to encourage you to switch back to us?
- Have your purchases stayed the same, decreased or increased in the last 12 months?
- Has your budget for next year been increased, stayed the same or been decreased for next year?
- Any other comments or is there anything I've missed?

See also:

Q70   Where can we get marketing help?

Q72   How do we revitalise our business?

Q84   How do we survey potential clients?

When contacting potential clients in a survey, it is important not to sell to them. Response rates to surveys of potential clients are lower than calling existing or lapsed clients. They may not be aware of the company name and also may not be keen to divulge too much information.

A survey call is not a sales call. It is important to keep the two separate, although the survey will provide useful information for the marketing team.

Questions for potential clients:

- Do you currently buy (this type of services or products)?
- How frequently do you buy these products or services – daily / weekly / monthly / quarterly / annually?
- How many of these do you use – daily / weekly / monthly / quarterly / annually?
- Do you have a specific selection criteria or accreditation process?
- Do you use any other company for these (services or products)?
- How long have you worked with (competitor name)?
- What do you like about (competitor name)?
- What do you dislike about (competitor name)?
- What change is likely to have a benefit on your company (other than pricing)?
- Have your purchases stayed the same, decreased or increased in the last 12 months?
- Has your budget for next year been increased, stayed the same or been decreased for next year?

- Any other comments or is there anything I've missed?

See also:

Q17 What's in a client proposal?

Q79 How can we win more pitches?

Q85   How do we survey our staff?

When conducting surveys, we often forget our staff. Companies survey customers, business leaders and industry associations, but staff are somehow forgotten. A staff survey is useful when a company is going through changes, before a company makes changes and when creating its marketing plan.

Start by exploring how much they understand about the business and then move on to ask questions about the individual.

<u>About our business:</u>

1. Describe our clients or customers (types of companies, size of business etc).
2. In your opinion, are we doing a good job in servicing the customer?
3. What do you think our customers and suppliers think of us?
4. Do you notice a difference in sales at certain times of the year? (if Yes, describe.)
5. How is our business different from last year?
6. If you ran the company for a day, what would you change?
7. Do you have any suggestions or ideas for the business?

<u>About you:</u>

8. Why are you working here?
9. What do you like about your role and working here?
10. What do you dislike about your role and working here?
11. Are there any areas you would like to improve on personally?
12. What other job would you like to do in this business?
13. What do you consider to be your main attributes that contribute to the company?

14. What training or skills development is required to improve your effectiveness?

15. Please add any other comments or observations.

We use **surveymonkey.com** for staff surveys. This provides an online survey template, which is free at the basic level. It also allows answers to be anonymous, which means you are more likely to get higher responses from staff.

HINT Always say 'thank you' for survey contributions, whether they are positive or negative.

See also:

Q32 How do we get the staff involved?

www.surveymonkey.com

Q86   How do focus groups work?

A focus group is a targeted group of people who may be potential or existing customers. They are gathered together, typically four to 12 at a time, to have an in-depth conversation about specific issues. Focus groups are used when you want or need:

- Feedback about existing products or services.
- Greater understanding of how / why customers buy your product.
- To test a product concept.
- Ideas to solve a specific challenge.
- Opinions about your service.

Sometimes, those involved in a focus group are rewarded. The reward may be financial, keeping samples, or simply holding the event in an interesting venue. Sometimes, you need more information after the meeting, such as asking the participants to try a product for a few weeks and to record their comments.

To organise your focus group:

- Develop the questions for which you need answers.
- Identify whether any props are needed, such as product samples.
- Ask someone to facilitate or lead the meeting. This person is known as the 'moderator' and should be someone with training or experience, so they do not lead the participants in the wrong direction.
- Make sure they have a list of questions that you need to be answered.
- Decide how the participants will be recruited.

The moderator will lead the group, make everyone feel at ease and ensure that all participants are involved in the discussions. The whole event usually lasts for 90 minutes to two hours.

See also:

Q70   Where can we get marketing help?

Q87   How do we measure service quality?

Q87   How do we measure service quality?

Buying services is different from buying products. The buying behaviour process for services involves need recognition and problem awareness, information search, evaluation of alternatives, purchase and post-purchase evaluation. With services, if they go wrong, customers often blame themselves for making a poor decision rather than blaming the service provider for a poor service!

Measuring service quality depends on perceptions and expectations. The *expected service* is what the client believes they will receive and is related to factors such as the branding of the organisation, the importance of the building where the service is delivered and the price; the *perceived service* is the service the client believes they have received.

The SERVQUAL model was designed as a framework to measure service quality by Parasuraman & Zeithamal. An adapted version is shown here:

Model element	Details
Responsiveness	Helpfulness and willingness of staff to deliver information and a quick service.
Tangibles	Evidence client can see to help anticipate the service they will receive.
Empathy	Considerate behaviour and attention directed towards the client, delivering information when promised.
Reliability	Delivery of the service as detailed or promised.
Assurance	Staff promoting trust and instilling confidence within the client that they will receive what they pay for.

You can measure your service delivery with a client survey, using a scale of 1 to 4, with 1 being low and 4 being high.

Model element	Questions for your clients
Responsiveness	On a scale of 1 to 4, how helpful were our staff when you initially contacted us or asked for information?
Tangibles	On the same scale, how do you rate our website / brochure?
Empathy	On the same scale, how do you rate the service once you had placed your order?
Reliability	On the same scale, how do you rate the actual delivery of the service?
Assurance	On the same scale, how do you rate our company as a whole, now that the service has been delivered?

This provides a maximum score of 20 and will enable you to decide where improvements are needed.

See also:

Q82 How do we survey existing clients?

Q86 How do focus groups work?

Q88   How do we maximise our presence at exhibitions?

Hosting or participating in an event or having a stand at an exhibition requires investment. Most of the work should be done in advance, so that everything runs smoothly on the day.

Before the Event (Planning)

Before the event, it is essential to agree the objectives of the event. These may include:

- Increasing sales, by finding a certain number of leads which will be converted into clients.
- Demonstrating new products to many people at once.
- Meeting prospective buyers who have been difficult to get appointments with.
- Launching a new service.
- A flag-waving event to promote the company.
- Keeping up with the competitors.
- An event to promote a new company name or service.
- A gathering of existing clients as a 'thank you'.

Once the objectives have been agreed, the next stage is to plan the event and decide the budget and identify other events taking place at the same time, so that your event doesn't clash. Also think about the factors that will make your event a real success.

Prepare a detailed action plan, identifying all tasks to be completed, when they need to be completed by, as well as by whom. Get regular updates to make sure some jobs don't get forgotten.

During the Event (Managing)

Staff should be smartly dressed in the corporate colours and with their names displayed. A smile is always useful too! Arrive early and make sure everything needed is in place. If people visit your stand, ask for their details – this sounds obvious but rarely happens. Wear a flower in your buttonhole! It breaks the ice and people always ask 'Where's the wedding!', providing the opportunity for you to start a conversation with them.

After the Event (Maximising)

Write 'thank you' letters to everyone who helped (they could be a future client) and make contact with all leads. Send out a letter (planned in advance), posting it immediately after the event is finished. Make sure the leads are sorted according to urgency and are contacted as soon as possible.

HINT Webinars and open days are alternatives to exhibitions.

See also:

Q42 How does sales promotion work?

Q67 How do we organise open days?

Q69 How do we get staff uniforms on a budget?

Q89 What are webinars?

Q89   What are webinars?

Webinars are online and interactive seminars. You need internet access and the ability to use your PC to connect to other PCs online. Led by one or more presenters, attendees can see the presentation live on their own PC screen. Questions can be submitted and answered either by telephone or in a space on their screen.

In practical terms, you need to visit a specific website, and enter a password and user name to gain access to the webinar. You often need to telephone another number, using your telephone system to gain access to conversations taking place.

Advantages of webinars

- You participate from your own office so no travel is needed.
- The event starts minutes before, so no lengthy registration processes are involved.
- They can be recorded and sent to other participants after the event.

The presentation must be slick, well-prepared and tested before going live.

Why would we use webinars?

They can be used to:

- Launch new products to agents or distributors at the same time.
- Share knowledge or information with a group who are spread out across a wide area.
- Include a sales team that may only get together once a year.
- Educate customers over a period of time.

Existing clients, as well as potential clients, can be invited to participate in your webinars.

See also:

Q62   How do we organise an email campaign?

Q90   How do we run webinars?

Q90   How do we run webinars?

The following companies offer webinar services through their software, for which there is a charge: **www.wiredred.co.uk**; **www2.gotomeeting.com**; and **www.webex.com**.

Sign up with one of these companies and then prepare your seminar – as PowerPoint slides, a short movie, a document or spreadsheet. If everyone has fast internet connections, it can be a combination of these items.

Before the webinar:

- Spend time getting the presentation ready.

- If using more than one presenter, agree who does what in advance.

- Set a start time and include a 10-minute preparation time.

- Send an agenda beforehand, so participants know what you will cover.

- Email everyone with a weblink to the webinar, a note of the telephone number, the time, user name, password and other information they may need.

- An hour beforehand, send out a quick reminder of what time they need to connect – and the telephone number.

- Get everyone connected 10 minutes before the start time to make sure everyone can get online OK.

During the webinar:

- Make sure the presenter has a clear voice.

- Give everyone guidelines on how the webinar will work.

- Let them know what to do if their system crashes, etc.

- If there are fewer than six people involved, ask the participants to introduce themselves (name and company and what they are looking to gain from the webinar).
- Explain how questions work (click on 'raise hand' button) and state name and question.
- Make sure presenter confirms participants' names or it is confusing for others.
- Tell people how long it will take.
- Ask if there is anything in particular they would like to cover.
- Don't just read the words on the screen, as all participants can see the screen easily.
- Keep it short! A series of short webinars is better than one long one.

HINT

Consider having two presenters instead of one, to change the voice in the mix.

See also:

Q88 How do we maximise our presence at exhibitions?

Q89 What are webinars?

Q91   What is interactive marketing?

Interactive or digital marketing involves:

- Video.
- Viral (**Q40**).
- Website (**Q50, Q51**).
- Social networks (**Q53**).
- Mobile or SMS (**Q57**).
- Email (**Q62**).
- Search engine optimisation (**Q92**).
- Google Adwords (**Q95**).
- Affiliate (**Q96**).

Interactive marketing tools can be turned on and off to enable you to manage orders. They can be sent at specific times on certain days as needed, and can include or exclude certain messages to reflect stock levels and peak season delivery times.

Mobile or SMS

SMS is powerful and can be used at the point of sale like no other interactive marketing tool. It can be used to identify customers who are not currently known to a company.

For example, a DIY store has a group of customers who pay 'cash' for items and thus do not leave a purchase history record, as they are not required to provide their contact details. To rectify this, a sign was posted on the trade counter of the DIY store asking customers to text 'DIYDISCOUNT' to a text number to receive a 10% discount off their order. The code received back had to be shown to the cashier so that the discount could be taken off. This allowed future offers and updates about stock to be sent to the mobile user, improving sales, customer engagement, retention and word of mouth marketing to reinforce brand products and services. Further SMS messages were forwarded to other members of the building trade. The promotion was easily measured through the number of SMS text messages received from different mobile numbers.

Video

Now cheaper and more accessible than it was (e.g., Flip Video Ultra Camcorder under £100), video gives businesses control of the messages they wish to communicate. Videos can be posted online on dedicated news sites or alternative sites like YouTube.

See also:

Q56 How can we use YouTube?

www.amazon.co.uk/exec/obidos/ASIN/B0018RPRCK/400001303-21/?m=A3P5ROKL5A1OLE

www.theflip.com

Q92   What is search engine optimisation?

Search engine optimisation (SEO) involves improving the volume and quality of traffic to a web site from search engines via 'natural' search results. Search engines need to see that a site is relevant to what someone is searching for.

Ways to optimise your website for search engines include:

- Do not construct your website using frames.
- Do not construct your website entirely in Flash.
- Use the TITLE tags thoughtfully – e.g., add keywords rather than 'home page'.
- Add appropriate text, including keywords to the ALT and TITLE tags attached to photos.
- Register with country-specific search engines.
- Put your web address on everything.
- Try to find a unique quality about your website and promote this.
- Link to other sites and have them link to your site.

And, in the end, if your website is well-constructed, it may simply need better promotion.

> **HINT** There are many companies that provide search engine optimisation services. Do get references, as many promise the earth but deliver little.

See also:

Q49   Why is our website not listed with search engines?

Q50   How do we get more website traffic?

Q51   How do we revamp our website?

Q93 What is micro-blogging?

Micro-blogging is a service that allows users to post status updates or 'tweets' by text, email or through websites – a way of sending instant messages to a specific group of people, wherever you are. You can 'follow' other users and be 'followed' in return. The best known micro-blogging site is **Twitter**, which limits a 'post' to 140 characters.

It has uses for both businesses and individuals but the PR people spotted its potential for getting onto the radar of influential people. Many politicians use Twitter – for example, Barack Obama is 'followed' on Twitter by over 200,000 people. Other micro-blog services include **Jaiku**, which launched in 2006 and is now a part of **Google**. Applications for Twitter have been created for the Apple iPhone, which increased the number of Twitter users.

Who uses Twitter?

- Politicians.
- People at conferences commenting about the speakers.
- People staying in touch with their fans or 'followers'.
- People wanting to comment about a new item.

How can my business use micro-blogging?

If your target audience is under 30 years old, they may already be following people on Twitter and you may need to get involved. You may want to identify competitors using Twitter and you might want to talk about events you're involved with.

See also:

Q20 What is a blog?

twitter.com

www.jaiku.com

Q94   How do we create case studies?

Case studies showcase work that you have done for a client. It's about the client explaining why they selected your company and how it helped their business.

A structured case study makes life easier and ensures that key questions are not forgotten. Face to face or over the telephone are the best ways to develop case studies. Questions might include:

Introduction questions – to get the respondent feeling comfortable, none of these are too difficult:

- When did (client) first begin working with (company)?
- Why did you choose (company)?
- How did you first hear about (company)?

We like to know something about our competitors, so we ask:

- How many other companies did (client) consider before selecting (company)?
- Why was (our company) better?

We re-visit the initial aims and explore the added value we have delivered:

- What did (client) initially want to achieve by using (company)?
- Have these aims been achieved, how?
- Have you achieved other things that you hadn't originally considered? If so, what?
- Can you give any figures or percentages of how business or customers have increased since using (company's) services?
- What do you particularly like or value about (company's) services to you?

These questions give us some measurements to see exactly how effective your work has been. You can then use these case studies to present to potential clients, in your newsletters, on the website and as press releases.

| HINT | We usually get someone who has not been involved with the project to make the call – that way any potential bias is removed. |

See also:

Q59 What should we include in newsletters?

Q64 How do we write press releases?

Q95   Does Google AdWords work?

Google is a search engine that searches for content online. **Adwords** is part of Google and is a paid-for search service also known as 'keyword advertising'. Adverts are triggered by the word the user searches for in Google, which means that it is a very focused form of advertising.

Google Adwords is available in different formats: text which is the most common form of ad; image; animated; mobile; and local business, where you focus on a specific geographical area. Ads include a promotional message and a link to your website, so it is aimed at businesses selling products online.

There are three main benefits of AdWords compared to traditional advertising:

- Reach: Based on the large number of internet users, AdWords is a way to communicate with potential customers outside your normal target market.

- Cost: There is no minimum spending limit, which means you can test keywords to see how they work. You can also set a monthly spending limit, say €50. You only pay for clicks through from your ad. In the past, people worried about competitors clicking their ad to waste their monthly budget, these are known as 'invalid clicks'. Google has introduced filtering technology to block 'invalid clicks'.

- Flexibility: You can trial keywords, change them and access your AdWords account at any time of the day.

Google AdWords works for many businesses, but you need to start with your website. When someone clicks through, where will they arrive? Will the site encourage a sale? Our experience is that, for specialised search terms, or in a smaller geographical area, AdWords can be very successful but they take time to set up and to refine.

HINT	Don't forget to calculate the cost per lead. If it's costing you €1 per click through for a €10 product, you need to check whether it's right for you. If it costs €1 for a €150 product where you don't have too many competitors, AdWords could work well.

See also:

Q51   How do we revamp our website?

Q78   How can we find new markets?

www.google.com/adwords/learningcenter

Q96   What are affiliate schemes?

Affiliates are people who own a website and advertise your products for sale on it. To start an affiliate scheme, you need to find an affiliate package. There are many – for example, **www.affiliatefuture.co.uk** and **www.affiliatewindow.com**. There is normally a fee for using such packages.

A suitable affiliate would be someone that owns a website (preferably one of high quality). The potential affiliate would go to your website where they can click on a link that you have added to your site to allow them to join your affiliate programme or go to an affiliate package provider's website (for example, Affiliatefuture) and choose merchants here.

Affiliates can sign up free and earn commission on every product purchased through their site. The commission rates vary depending on the volume of products sold. Typically, these rates are from 5% to 20%, while some pay a flat fee of say €10, depending on the value generated for the company.

See also:

Q91   What is interactive marketing?

Q97 Do golf days work?

Golf days are seen as a way of doing business and, in our experience, they work. People buy from people and the best way to get to know each other is when you're confined in a space together. A golf course or other event is a good way to spend time getting to know someone and understanding their needs. Golf days can be an alternative to an exhibition.

The general rule of thumb is that the one discussion that you do not start is about the client's business. Let them have a good day rather than feel pressured into talking about business. The first stage is finding out whether or not you want to do business together. If the chemistry and the opportunity is there, you may get a call later.

You can either piggy-back on another golf day and enter a team or you could organise your own golf day. Either way, it's usually 18 holes of golf followed by an evening meal and presentation. To build up the 'team spirit', there are often competitions, which may include nearest the pin, longest drive, best individual score, best team score and much more!

Here's a suggested schedule for your own golf day:

Time	Activity
11:45 am	Registration opens, sandwiches and hot drinks
12:20 pm	Player briefing
12.30 pm	Tee off
5:00 pm	After game drinks
6.00 pm	Evening dinner

HINT
Attend a few golf days before organising your own.
Consider partnering with another company to run a joint golf day and share the work.

See also:

Q39 How does sponsorship work for smaller businesses?

Q88 How do we maximise our presence at exhibitions?

Q89 What are webinars?